THE EARLY WORDSWORTHIAN MILIEU

A Notebook of Christopher Wordsworth
with a few entries by
William Wordsworth

EDITED BY

Z. S. FINK

OXFORD
AT THE CLARENDON PRESS
1958

c

PRINTED IN GREAT BRITAIN
AT THE UNIVERSITY PRESS, OXFORD
BY CHARLES BATEY, PRINTER TO THE UNIVERSITY

To

MY WIFE

PREFACE

THE justification for presenting to the reader the notebook in this volume does not lie in any intrinsic literary merit which it possesses; nor in its being mainly in William Wordsworth's hand, for his contributions are few; nor in new sources of his poetry which it uncovers; but primarily in the circumstance that, through following leads given by the notations of his brother Christopher, we are led to a closer view of William's early reading than we have previously had. Since the general subject of his sources and analogues has been treated by a long succession of scholars from Lienemann to Abbie Findlay Potts, I have made no attempt to resurvey it in the introductory essay. Instead, writing with an informed consciousness of their findings, I have confined myself to specific points raised by the notebook entries and have attempted only to make appropriate observations about them.

I wish to express my thanks to Miss Helen Darbishire, who facilitated my access to materials which I could not otherwise have seen and answered my questions with unfailing patience; Dr. Franklyn B. Snyder, President Emeritus of Northwestern University, who immediately appreciated the importance of the notebook; Mr. Jens Nyholm, who called my attention to the collection in which the notebook was found; and the Rev. William Arthur Wordsworth, who kindly gave me permission to print the 'Outline of a Poem descriptive of the lakes' now in the British Museum. I am also under obligation to Deans Payson S. Wild, Simeon E. Leland, and Moody E. Prior, and to Professors Arthur Tebbutt, Frederic E. Faverty, Burton Milligan, Bergen Evans, Clyde Murley, Frank Brown, and Walter B. Rideout. I have been assisted in innumerable ways by the staffs of the

British Museum, the Library of St. John's College, Cambridge, the Museum at Grasmere, the Library of Congress, the Library Company of Philadelphia, and the Houghton, Morgan, New York Public, Yale, Cornell, Wellesley, Huntington, Northwestern, Newberry, and Illinois Libraries. Mr. H. M. Adams and Mr. A. Halcrow, Librarian and Sub-Librarian of Trinity College, Cambridge, at considerable personal inconvenience facilitated my examination of the library's large collection of the papers of Christopher Wordsworth. Lady Hester Pinney let me examine the Racedown Inventory, and Miss Catharine Marshall gave me access to Dorothy Wordsworth's early letters to Jane Pollard. Inspector Fred G. Bennett of the Evanston Police gave me technical assistance. Two professional examiners of handwriting were employed to make independent examinations of the notebook.

The fact that the collection in which the notebook was found contained two notes addressed to a Mr. Wise, who can only be identified as Thomas J. Wise, made necessary an extended investigation of it. The notes are very brief and both are concerned with Wise's *Bibliography of the Writings in Prose and Verse of William Wordsworth,* one acknowledging receipt of copies of it and the other expressing the opinion that some of the writing illustrated opposite p. 171, identified by Wise as that of Dorothy Wordsworth, was actually that of Sarah Hutchinson. Both notes are signed by Gordon Wordsworth, grandson of the poet. Rigorous examination uncovered no evidence that any document in the collection was spurious, and led to the conclusion that the appearance of Wise's name was significant only as possibly indicating that the documents may once have been in his possession, as were a great many other things of undoubted authenticity.

With the exception of the *Guide to the Lakes,* all Wordsworth's works edited by de Selincourt are referred to in his editions unless otherwise noted, the conventional abbreviations *E.L.*, *M.Y.*, and *L.Y.* being employed to designate the three divisions into which his edition of the *Letters* falls. For the other prose works I have used the edition of William Knight. Unless there is indication to the contrary, *The Prelude* is referred to in the text of 1805–6; *An Evening Walk* and *Descriptive Sketches* are regularly cited in the versions of 1793. Dorothy's *Journals* are referred to in de Selincourt's edition. The short title *Memoirs* designates the *Memoirs of William Wordsworth* by his nephew Christopher. In so far as it has been possible to identify them, all works cited in the notebook are referred to in the Essay and Notes, except when notice is given to the contrary, in the editions cited in the entries. For a list of these the reader is referred to p. 75. The abbreviation Np. is used to indicate a reference to a page in the notebook. Three accompanying loose sheets are cited by abbreviations such as L1r.; that is, Leaf 1 *recto*. An explanation of the editorial apparatus employed in printing the transcription of the notebook will be found in the note preceding the text. Except when I write in my own person I have made no attempt to regularize the spelling of Lake district proper names.

Z. S. F.

Evanston, Illinois

15 *March* 1958

CONTENTS

ILLUSTRATIONS

THE ESSAY

On a grey December day I sat in the office of Mr. Jens Nyholm, Librarian of Northwestern University, looking over some documents which a New York bookseller had described as 'Wordsworth Family Papers', and which we had asked him to send us for examination. He had put them in a large manila envelope and dispatched them through the mails without cardboard or other protection. Neither we nor the dealer expected much.

For the most part what we found answered our expectations. The papers were mainly letters written by various members of the Wordsworth family from 1836 to 1911 which had apparently been preserved in the family of the Rev. Henry Michell Wagner, vicar of Brighton, who married Mary Sykes Watson, daughter of Joshua Watson, the philanthropist. There were also a book of not very good Lake district sketches, later than 1840, and two notebooks. The larger of these contained opinions of William Wordsworth on men, politics, and poetry which were taken down by his nephew Christopher during a holiday visit to Rydal Mount about 1834-5 and from which, it was apparent, were drawn many of the views attributed to the poet in the *Memoirs* of 1851.

It was with the feeling that Christopher's jottings probably constituted the major piece of the collection that I picked up the remaining notebook. Presently, as Lake Michigan outside the window became more and more shrouded in the dusky obscurity of the winter's day, I found myself reading of mists and fogs by other shores and of winter pleasures of long ago on other lakes—of 'scaiting' on Esthwaite and of Hawkshead, and discovered that I was in the world out of which came the poetry of William Wordsworth.

The notebook which produced these unexpected results is a thin little one measuring four by six inches, with a number of cut-out and missing leaves but with ten remaining which are covered on both sides with entries, and with three loose accompanying sheets of various sizes, one and possibly two of which appear to have been retrieved from the unused portions of old letters. The entries are made without margin, a fact which here and there creates problems in reading, for the outer edges are somewhat frayed. A consecutive series of numbers is attached to certain entries and runs through them from front to back. No apparent plan emerges when these notations are read in order, however, and the grouping of them by subjects on L1r., and L3r., together with variations in the ink, suggests that the numbers were added later and that their purpose was to assist the writer in locating entries containing materials on certain poetic themes in which he was interested. There is no more order in the other entries, which are consecutive neither from page to page nor, often, from the top of a page to the bottom. Variations in the handwriting and in the colours to which the ink has aged and the employment of different quills show that the notations were made at different times. Repeated interlinear additions and a persistent habit of avoiding hyphenation by jamming letters together at the end of a line add to the complexity. On the inside of the back cover the notations include 'Wordsworth', 'Wordswo', and two flourishes beginning with a capital W and continuing with a series of o's. More than one hand is present.

We may make progress in disentangling this chaos by observing, first, that at an undeterminable date a child scribbled on the insides of both covers and on a number of pages. As the stubs show, leaves which were thus spoiled for further use were later cut out, leaving those which were blank or largely so. The identity of the writer cannot be determined, and we shall have no further occasion to refer to his activities.

The remaining notations may be divided into two groups. One consists of a series of related passages on pp. 1, 5, 11, 13, and 19. Though it is by no means certain that they have a common subject, indications are strong that they all revolve around a tale in which two armed knights confront each other, one of whom is apparently the father, and the other the suitor, of a fair maiden. They are also distinguished by all appearing at the top of pages and by all containing attempts at expanded similes which in style and manner remind us at once of Milton. There is considerable variation in the hand, but it is of the sort readily explicable in terms of the common explanations of differences in the writing of a single person. All the entries exhibit the characteristic features of the early hand of William Wordsworth, and are unquestionably in his holograph.[1]

How exactly can we determine the date at which these entries were made? The infusion of Lake district images into Miltonic forms which they exhibit appears also—and in a somewhat more developed form, though not in that of the expanded simile—in 'The Dog: An Idyllium' (1786?), written during the Hawkshead schooldays, a circumstance which may lead us to suspect that they go back to the very beginnings of Wordsworth's literary activity. The evidence is considerable that this is in fact the case.

We begin with a passage in *The Prelude* in which we are told of a time in his boyhood or early youth when first his ears

---

[1] Particularly significant in comparing the entries with known specimens of Wordsworth's hand are the distinctive capitals E, H, and T; the small x, y, and k; the f with only an upper loop or with no loop; the frequent separation of initial s from the following part of a word; and the tendency to finish a final e, d, and some other letters with an upstroke beginning before the preceding downstroke has reached the bottom of the word.

> began to open to the charm
> Of words in tuneful order, found them sweet
> For *their own sakes*, a passion and a power;
> And phrases pleas'd me, chosen for delight,
> For pomp, or love.

(v. 577–81)

He goes on to tell of morning walks by the still borders of Esthwaite Water when for two hours at a time he and a schoolfellow who shared his interests would spout favourite verses. It is reasonable to suppose that this awakening to the beauty and power of words immediately preceded his own attempts at composition and led naturally into them, and that before poems came fragments of poems and incipient attempts at literary creation in both prose and verse. Wordsworth dates these developments in the 1850 text as occurring when he was 'twice five years or less', but in the 1805–6 version he mentions the age of thirteen, and this accords more closely with the other evidence, for the school exercise which constitutes his earliest complete poem was written in 1784–5 to commemorate the bicentenary of Hawkshead School, and in 'The Idiot Boy' he specifically places the beginning of his poetic career at fourteen.

Evidence that the entries in Group I are among these earliest attempts at composition, and that they belong to the period which he indicates, is at hand. From the same passage in *The Prelude* in which he tells us of the development of his love of words and phrases, we learn something about the poems of which he was enamoured at the time. In *The Recluse* we are told of an early boyish passion for tales of conflicts, battles, warriors, and duels to the death.[1] From his letters and his first published poem we learn of an interest in the poetry of Helen Maria Williams.[2] Echoes in other

---

[1] i. 703–50.
[2] See *E.L.*, pp. 66–67, and the 'Sonnet on Seeing Miss Helen Maria Williams Weep at a Tale of Distress', which appeared in the *European Magazine* for February 1787, not in the March issue as is often stated.

his crest waded dreadful in
his head likean oak on the left
shook by the wind upon
the top of Teneriff

As when the moon ... the
cover she beholdabove the How?
asts upon the Branches as...
tall oak, which grows ...
the summit of the Top is

o love cod and mor

mek EGE EP

description ... which fell at
Loudore bankes & blocked up the pas-
age into Borrowdale. Grays Journal
f. 283. 9 l.

Loudore waterfall 11

Description of an evening f. 206. G. Let
& Night.

Notebook, page 5

early poems tell us that he also admired Thomas Gray, and it is reasonable to suppose that he encountered William Mason, whose edition of Gray had appeared in 1776 and may have led him to Mason's own works. If we put these bits of evidence together, it is not difficult to surmise that the poems in which he delighted when poetic phrases first were sweet to him were such things as Miss Williams's pseudo-ballad *Edwin and Eltruda* (1782), a tale of distress indeed in which a baron who dwelt by Derwent's side is killed in battle by his daughter's suitor, and Mason's dramatic poem *Elfrida* (1752), which had an enormous vogue at the time of its appearance and steady editions in succeeding decades, and which tells of the bitter enmity between Elfrida's father and her husband and a fatal duel between the latter and King Edgar. Perhaps one should add, too, some of the other 'Edwin and' poems of the century, such as those of Mallet and Goldsmith, and Hoole's translation of Tasso (1763), a copy of which Wordsworth is reputed to have joined other boys in giving to Hawkshead School. Now when we turn to the series of similes in the notebook, it is obvious that such poems would contribute, along with Milton, to suggest exactly the kind of situations which we find in them, and it is further to be observed that in the entry on Np. 19 Wordsworth not only uses the name of Mason's heroine, a circumstance significant in the light of his notorious lack of originality in inventing names, but selects one which by syllabic equivalence and its very sound suggests Miss Williams's Eltruda.

We have, then, evidence that Wordsworth as a boy of fourteen or thereabouts was captivated by the pseudo-medievalism of the day, we can identify with reasonable certainty some of the poems that enthralled him, and the similes in the notebook turn on such situations as these poems suggest.

But we have yet further testimony to the very early period to which the entries in Group I belong, for they represent

5

more than simply Miss Williams or Mason or even Tasso Miltonized by Wordsworth. In one of them is an image with a fascinating history which can be traced in detail and which has chronological significance. In Book IV of *The Prelude* the poet tells us of his return during the first summer vacation of his college years to

> That lowly bed whence I had heard the wind
> Roar, and the rain beat hard, where I so oft
> Had lain awake on summer's nights to watch
> The moon in splendour couched among the leaves
> Of a tall ash, that near our cottage stood;
> Had watched her with fixed eyes while to and fro
> In the dark summit of the waving tree
> She rocked with every impulse of the breeze.
> (1850, ll. 85–92)

These lines not only take us back to an observation of Wordsworth's schooldays, but I think no one will be disposed to question that they present a variant of the image which, as it was originally recorded in the notebook on p. 5, read as follows:

> As when the moon as she
>   when she [?]   [?]
> raises her orb above the Horizon
> rests upon the Branches of some
> tall ash, which grows upon
> the summit of the Horizon

But the ash in this entry did not long remain an ash, for Wordsworth presently cancelled it by writing 'oak' over it. Why, we may ask, did this transformation occur? The answer is to be found in the fact that the image not only centres attention on the moon but also contains the suggestion of a tree standing out against the horizon in the light of a heavenly body, and that this reminded him of another image he had observed, either before or after making the original entry—that of an oak standing sharply against the horizon at sunset—which he later used in both his first long poem *The Vale of Esthwaite* (1787):

> While in the west the robe of day
> Fades, slowly fades, from gold to gray,
> The oak its boughs and foliage twines
> Mark'd to the view in stronger lines.
>
> (ll. 95–98)

and *An Evening Walk* (1793):

> And fronting the bright west in stronger lines,
> The oak its dark'ning boughs and foliage twines.
>
> (ll. 193–4)

Commenting on the history of this image in the Fenwick note to the latter poem, Wordsworth said:

> This is feebly and imperfectly expressed, but I recollect distinctly the very spot where this first struck me. It was in the way between Hawkshead and Ambleside, and gave me extreme pleasure. The moment was important in my poetical history; for I date from it my consciousness of the infinite variety of natural appearances which had been unnoticed by the poets of any age or country, so far as I was acquainted with them; and I made a resolution to supply, in some degree, the deficiency.

Then he added: 'I could not have been at that time above fourteen years of age.' Unreliable as the Fenwick notes may be in the dating of his poems, still they cannot always be wrong, and what this note says about the beginning of his career is corroborated, as we have seen, by other testimony and corroborates that testimony as well. The statement takes us straight to 1784–5, toward which all the other evidence points.

Of course, it is true that the date at which a poet observes an image does not in itself establish that at which he makes even incipient literary use of it, and this is especially true of a writer as ruminative as Wordsworth. But even in such a case there has to be a time at the beginning of his career

7

when the observation of images and their use are close together. That in the notebook we are back at that time is a conclusion to which all the evidence points. Moreover, we are entitled to ask whether the observation of the ash did not occur before that of the oak which transformed it in the notebook entry. If so, we are indeed at the very beginning of Wordsworth's literary career.

Much that is observable in these early notations lasted, though not always constantly, in his later work. It is clear that what he began with was the expanded simile. The specimens in Group I must be regarded as his earliest prentice work in this form—as materials to be translated into poetic form in a boyish tale of love and battle. A later experiment using the same formula, though it is given a nautical setting, is printed by Miss Darbishire in the *Poetical Works*:

> As when, upon the smooth pacific deep
> Dense fogs, to sight impervious, have withheld
> Some gallant vessel from some bold Emprize
> Day after day deferred, till anxious hope
> Yields to despair, if chance a sudden breeze
> Spring up and dissipate the veil, all hearts
> Throb at the change, and every sail is spread
> To speed her course along the dazzling waves
> For recompense of glorious conquest soon
> To be atchieved upon the astonish'd foe.
>
> (v. 346)

The manner is assuredly not Wordsworth's most distinctive one, but he recurred to it in some rhetorically splendid passages in the Eighth, Ninth, and Tenth Books of *The Prelude*—passages which, if they are not typical Wordsworthian blank verse, are surely the most Miltonic lines outside Milton.

The ballad influence, too, at least in the form of the eighteenth-century pseudo-ballad, was with him from the start. In the light of the notebook entries, is it too much to suggest that the specific tale at which he imagined Miss Williams weeping in his earliest published poem was her own *Edwin and Eltruda*? Moreover, the basic situation in this poem of young lovers brought to grief by family and political difficulties recurs later in *Vaudracour and Julia*. It is curious that the works of this same Miss Williams also appear to have been drawn upon in this later poem.[1] One is prompted to ask whether this enigmatic tale, about the origins of which Wordsworth's own statements are so unsatisfactory, did not have its thematic origin in a boyish desire to write a poem of thwarted lovers in imitation of Miss Williams, a later model from her works superseding an earlier one, and other sources and his own experiences supplying modifying details until what finally resulted preserved only the most general thematic resemblance to what had been originally intended. I suggest that Wordsworth had the capacity to delight early in a theme, to carry it in his mind for years as a poetic intention, to give it expression at widely separated periods of time, and in the process finally to transform it to the point where the basic intention alone or even only traces of it survived.

There is another way in which the content of these early entries is significant. Their explicit documentation of Wordsworth's statements in *The Recluse* about his early delight in tales of martial clashes gives a new emphasis to the lines in *The Prelude* on his search for a suitable theme for a great long poem and to the long list of martial subjects which he considered. If this account reminds one irresistibly of Milton's 'long choosing' and turning from deeds of valour to higher themes, it was not simply due to Wordsworth's consciously imitating the older poet but arose also out of the circumstance that a very real parallel existed in his own experience. We cannot but believe that the military themes to which he alludes received, at some stage in the history of

---

[1] See F. M. Todd, 'Wordsworth, Helen Maria Williams, and France', in *MLR*, xliii (1948), 456–64. Wordsworth tried to see Miss Williams in Paris in 1792 and did see her there in 1820 (*E.L.*, pp. 66–67; *M.Y.*, pp. 903, 907).

his ambition to write a great long poem, a less perfunctory consideration than has sometimes been supposed.

Finally, what we have learned about the entries in Group I has its major importance in the fact that it has a bearing on the vexatious question of the autobiographical accuracy of *The Prelude* and on the way in which we should read that poem. In our sceptical age, it was both inevitable and necessary that the trust of an older generation in the faithfulness of the poem to the facts of Wordsworth's experience should come under attack. There is much in the notebook to support this revaluation, and we may grant that his memory was essentially creative, but the entries also point to a counterbalancing truth about the poem. We have discovered some striking corroborations of Wordsworth's statements in it which should make us ever remember that his mind was one which craved 'real things', and that the factual foundation on which he built was sometimes, at least, rather more solid than it has become the fashion to suppose.

All the other entries in the notebook may be placed in Group II. Most of them are clearly themes for poetic treatment set down without any discernible order. These entries were not written by William Wordsworth, and taken simply by themselves raise formidable problems of chronology and identification, for their relationships with his works are complex and they are not in the hand of any of the rather considerable number of scribes who wrote for him at different stages of his career. Fortunately, however, two manuscripts from the pen of his younger brother Christopher are available to assist in solving these difficulties, one a diary kept at Cambridge in 1793–4 and now in the Trinity College Library, the other an 'Outline of a Poem descriptive of the lakes', which the Rev. William Arthur Wordsworth, grandson of the Bishop of Lincoln, gave to the British Museum in 1945.[1] Comparison of the Northwestern notebook with these documents makes clear that the entries in Group II are

[1] Add. MS. 46136. For the text see the Appendix.

10

largely, if not entirely, in Christopher's hand. The fact also emerges that they consist of materials, jotted down at different times, for the Latin descriptive poem on the Lake district of which the 'Outline of a Poem' is an elaborated prose synopsis. We may surmise from both documents that some months before he entered Cambridge in the autumn of 1792 Christopher was envisaging a Latin poem. Perhaps he was already thinking in terms of a prize poem with which he would win distinction at the University. Some such production had apparently been expected from William, and there is evidence that there had been discontent on the part of their guardians at its failure to appear.[1]

These circumstances go far to establish an approximate date for the notebook entries. There is, however, additional evidence. Though it is an arresting fact that no work which appeared later than 1789 is anywhere referred to, and some of the oldest entries may belong to this period, most of the notations are certainly not so early. On Np. 16 we read of a storm which occurred in 1790. The greater part of the writing, moreover, represents a stage in the development of Christopher's hand, a rapidly evolving one in his earlier years, which is close to that in the 'Outline of a Poem'. On Np. 3 there is reference to a bishop's having planted an 'immense quantity' of oak trees near his 'new house'. The allusion is to Richard Watson, Bishop of Llandaff, a person who makes an appearance at several points in the Wordsworth history, and to Calgarth Park, not far from Ambleside on the eastern shore of Windermere, the foundations of which were laid in 1789. Writing in March 1807, the bishop tells us that sixteen years previously he had planted 200,000 oaks on a mountain near Ambleside.[2] Clearly referring to these same trees, Andrew Pringle says in 1797 that they had then had seven years' growth.[3] The slight discrepancy in the

---

[1] *Memoirs*, i. 14.
[2] *Miscellaneous Tracts* (London, 1815, 2 vols.), ii. 414.
[3] 'General View of the Agriculture of Westmoreland', in J. Bailey and

two accounts may be resolved if we assume that Watson was counting back from the last anniversary of the planting of the trees in the previous October and that Pringle was writing late in 1797 and counting back from that time. The two would then agree that the oaks were planted in the autumn of 1790. But it is at least equally likely that the bishop was being exact and Pringle slightly inaccurate. In this case we are led to the latter part of 1791 and the period immediately before the 'Outline of a Poem'.

Some entries, however, may not be quite so late, for on 23 May 1791 Dorothy records in a letter that Christopher was making a walking tour of the Lake district with two schoolfellows.[1] The Atkinson and Leeson of the notebook are probably the two schoolfellows, for though Leeson has disappeared, a John Atkinson of Dalton was a Hawkshead schoolboy and Cambridge contemporary of Christopher, who mentions him in the Trinity College diary on 26 and 28 October 1793. If more than one hand has to be admitted into the entries, the hypothesis of schoolboys making notations in a common notebook before, during, or after a walking tour supplies a ready explanation.

Much has been written about William Wordsworth's remarkable sister Dorothy and his sensitive brother John, but it has not been generally recognized that striking similarities of temperament and feeling also existed between William and Christopher. The mature careers of the two men diverged markedly. Yet there has long been available a good deal to suggest that for a time, at least, there were not two Wordsworths with but a single heart and soul, but three. It seemed to Dorothy that her favourite brother and her youngest one were much alike. In 1791 she wrote that Christopher's disposition was of the 'same cast' as William's and that his inclinations had taken the same turn;

G. Culley, *General View of the Agriculture of the County of Northumberland* (London, 1805, 3rd ed.), p. 319.
[1] *E.L.*, p. 45.

both, she declared, had a great attachment to poetry;[1] and in February 1793, just after Christopher had spent the Christmas vacation with her and they had prepared a long critique of William's *An Evening Walk* and *Descriptive Sketches*, she again found that he was 'like William', that he was 'no despicable Poet', that he had the 'same traits in his character', and that he was 'attached to the same pursuits which have so irresistible an Influence over William'.[2] We catch further glimpses of his early interest in poetry in the activities of a literary society to which he belonged at Cambridge, which included Coleridge, and of the meetings of which we read in his diary. William himself, moreover, may well have had Christopher particularly in mind in the following lines which were once apparently intended for inclusion in *The Prelude*:

> My playmates! brothers! nurs'd by the same years,
> And fellow-children of the self-same hills,
> Though we are moulded now by various fates
> To various characters, I do not think
> That there is one of us who cannot tell
> How manifold the expedients, how intense
> The unwearied passion with which nature toils
> To win us to herself, and to impress
> Our careless hearts with beauty and with love.
> <div align="right">(<i>Poets. Wks.</i> v. 346)</div>

The likelihood is heightened, at least, by the circumstance that the lines contain the same sentiment of similar early experiences and divergent walks in later life which is found in the stanzas 'To the Rev. Dr. Wordsworth', composed at Christmastide in 1819 to accompany *The River Duddon*.

There is therefore considerable external evidence to fill out the picture of the young Christopher's literary aims and ambitions which the notations in Group II give us. Yet though it is remarkable that some of the autobiographical

---

[1] *E.L.*, pp. 51–52.
[2] *E.L.*, p. 83.

entries contain anticipations of the tone of *The Prelude* more striking than anything we have from William himself at so early a date, and though there was no lack of intensity of response on Christopher's part, it is only too clear from the painfully pedestrian 'Outline of a Poem' that a vast difference existed between the two brothers in the capacity to transmute their feelings and materials into the forms of art. The real significance of the entries therefore resides less in what they tell us about Christopher than in the many relationships which exist between them and the works of his older brother. These are different in kind from those between the poems and Dorothy's *Journals*, but they are not for this reason less illuminating.

These relationships have several explanations. Assuming for the moment that William and Christopher were not together very much after William left Hawkshead, for their parents had died early and they had no home to draw to, their common school environment and similarities of temperament yet go far to account for similarities in the autobiographical entries. Beyond this the explanation is partly to be found in the fact that they shared a common literary store—that Christopher's literary milieu was also William's.

By the 1790's the loco-descriptive poem was a literary form which had been extensively practised in England for some decades and had acquired a well-developed set of conventions. There were also the descriptive themes of the eighteenth-century poets like Thomson, Goldsmith, and Beattie, many of them out of Virgil and Milton, and the episodic narratives with which they interspersed their lines. Then there were the anthologies, particularly the schoolbooks like G. Whitaker's *Florilegium Poeticum ex Ovidio, Tibullo, Propertio, Martiali etc.*, expurgated and published 'In usum tyronum', and Vicesimus Knox's *Elegant Extracts of Poetry*, which William later referred to as constituting the 'poetical library of our schools'.[1] Knox printed not only

---

[1] *Prose Wks.* iii. 176.

14

complete poems like Gray's *Elegy*, including a great many on popular themes by now forgotten writers, but also passages from the older poets which accorded with the taste of the time. Such books were powerful influences in moulding the literary tastes of several generations of schoolboys. Finally, there were the picturesque writers and along with them the writers of Lake district guide-books and 'surveys' like West and Clarke, who were already showing how the precepts of devotees of the picturesque and the generalized descriptive themes of earlier eighteenth-century poets could be applied to the Lake district. In view of the existence of this body of materials, we must conclude that William and Christopher to a very considerable extent drew the same things from common sources, a circumstance which in itself gives to the latter's notations their unique value as a guide to the poetic materials with which William worked in the early stages of his career.

But there are some entries which raise the question whether they can be fully accounted for on such a basis. On Np. 17 we find this notation:

> Oft have I watched with impatience the buds
> & the blossoms of spring, which when they had
> appeared, it delighted me to lead my wildly
> devious way. Along thy banks oh Winder. Conis.
> Esth. Gras. Rydal. Cas. etc.

The entry gives us not only the same kind of sentiment we find in William, but in at least one curious respect his very language, for 'devious' was a very special word with him, his constant one to describe, as here, the meanderings of a foot traveller. We find in the poems 'Opened at once and stayed my devious feet' (*E.W.*, 1849, l. 56); 'His devious course' (*Prel.*, 1850, viii. 209); 'a devious traveller' (ibid. ix. 447); 'By devious footsteps' (*Excur.* iv. 517); 'Nor need the windings of his devious course' (ibid. vi. 1087); and 'Alone and devious from afar he came' (*Recl.* i. 6). An even more remarkable verbal relationship is found in the following entry on Np. 7:

> In autumn misty evening, the shepherd stalking
> over the mountains, sees or thinks he sees mon-
> sters through the mists. Or rather you, if you
> should be set there take the shepherd for a
> giant.

The monsters of this passage are no doubt from Collins's
'Ode on the Superstitions of the Highlands of Scotland',
mentioned in a notation on L3r., but we also have echoes
from Milton's

> Faerie Elves,
> Whose midnight Revels, by a Forrest side
> Or Fountain, some belated peasant sees,
> Or dreams he sees
>
> (*P. L.* i. 781–4)

and from Thomson's

> Indistinct on earth,
> Seen through the turbid air, beyond the life
> Objects appear; and 'wildered, o'er the waste
> The Shepherd stalks gigantic.
>
> ('Autumn', ll. 722–5)

In separate passages but in the same book of *The Prelude*
both passages are echoed again:

> He looks and sees the cavern spread and grow,
> Widening itself on all sides, sees or thinks
> He sees, erelong *etc.*
>
> (viii. 714–16)

> or on rainy days
> When I have angled up the lonely brooks
> Mine eyes have glanced upon him, few steps off,
> In size a giant, stalking through the fog.
>
> (viii. 397–400)

The first of these passages, moreover, has a curious variation.
Milton wrote 'sees, / Or *dreams* he sees'; Wordsworth, not
only remembering, but after the fashion of the creative

imagination, remaking, but not alas! always improving, 'sees, or *thinks* / He sees'. And this verbal idiosyncracy, it will be observed, is also the reading of the entry in the notebook. It is one which occurs in no edition of *Paradise Lost*.

Entries such as these at least raise the question of the extent to which the two brothers may have worked together or echoed each other. There is a paucity of information about their movements, but some things we do know. William spent the summers of 1788 and 1789 in the Lake district, the time when, according to the traditional dating, he is supposed to have finished *An Evening Walk*, a work with which the notebook has an unusual number of relationships. In October 1789 he returned to Cambridge and was not again in the North until some time in 1793, having in the meantime spent the summer and early autumn of 1790 on the Continent and the latter part of 1791 and almost the whole of 1792 in France. Christopher, so far as we know, did not leave his native hills and valleys until he went to Cambridge in the autumn of 1792. It would therefore appear that, though the two must have been together at times during the summers of 1788 and 1789, they probably could not have met at any subsequent time within the period covered by the notebook. We might yet suppose, however, that during the summers when they did see each other, Christopher picked up a good deal from William in the way of themes, poems, and books affording useful models, and was aroused to emulation by his brother's plans. We might further believe that, thereafter, being a young man of little originality and invention, he followed closely in William's footsteps, though if he did so, it is clear that he did not work from any finished form of *An Evening Walk*, for what the notebook contains is not references to that work but materials of the sort out of which it was made.

There is in letters another possible explanation. None from this period between the two brothers survive, yet it is clear that as early as the middle of 1790 they were corresponding. In the well-known letter to Dorothy of 6 September of that year William remarks that Christopher would be surprised at not having heard from him because they were 'almost upon terms of a regular correspondence'. We know, too, that the lengthy critique of *An Evening Walk* and *Descriptive Sketches* which Christopher and Dorothy drew up during the Christmas vacation of 1792 was intended to be sent to William,[1] and the Trinity College diary shows the two brothers writing and Christopher deeply interested in William's literary endeavours. From these circumstances it seems reasonable to suggest that his development had been rapid, that upon the elder brother's return from the Continent in the autumn of 1790 an active correspondence may have sprung up between them in which there was a good deal of exchanging of interests, enthusiasms, and poetical themes, and that as a result they perhaps possessed a store of such things which was common not only in the sense that it came from common origins and feelings but also in that it was shared between them. The likelihood that this was the case is increased, moreover, by an obvious common interest in the picturesque which they had at the time—William originally intended to call *Descriptive Sketches* (1791–2) *Picturesque Sketches*, as he tells us in a note to the poem— and by the fact that *An Evening Walk*, a poem with many connexions with the notebook, clearly had not yet reached any final form, for even in 1794, after it was published, he still thought of it as in some sense unfinished and worked actively at revising it.[2] Commonly supposed on the basis of a Fenwick note to have been finished in 1789, we may well suspect that it was one of the literary endeavours at which William was at least desultorily at work during the very period when Christopher was planning his Latin poem.

So far circumstance and conjecture take us in determining the early literary relations of the two men. Whatever they may have been, the connexions between Christopher's

[1] *E.L.*, pp. 85–86. [2] *E.L.*, p. 116.

18

jottings and William's works remain, and they possess a significance which is quite independent of any explanation of why they exist. To the exploration of these we may now turn.

The Vale of Esthwaite

The Vale of Esthwaite, the first extended expression of Wordsworth's persistent topographical urge, was composed during the spring and summer of 1787 while he was spending his last months in Hawkshead as a schoolboy. Long supposed to have been lost, it survives in part in three early manuscripts which together give us something over five hundred of the 'many hundreds' of lines of which it consisted. Though it antedates Christopher's entries, it clearly grew out of the same general body of materials and many of the same responses and feelings. On Np. 1, for example, we find this entry:

> Oft have I walked till the
> golden redness in the west faded
> into the sober gray of the
> evening, & even till twilight

and in ll. 95–96 of the poem:

> While in the west the robe of day
> Fades, slowly fades, from gold to gray.

And with Christopher's notation on Np. 18

> I have felt along thy banks, what time
> at Eve in the spring, the birds etc. When
> the horizon was contracting, & the soft
> shour yet hanging dubious, which
> conferred a kindly gloom, O Esthwaite
> sensations, such as would that I
> might often feel

19

we may compare ll. 75–78:

> Lone wandering oft by Esthwaite's s[tream]
> My soul has felt the mystic drea[m],
> When Twilight, wrapp'd in dusky s[hroud],
> Slow journey'd from her cave of cloud.

The poem opens, moreover, with morning, noon, and night scenes, the same Miltonic scheme of arrangement which figures so prominently in Christopher's plans.

Evening, as we learn from entries on Npp. 3, 7, 13, 14, and 16, was also the time for supernatural appearances and for tales of such phenomena. We need not be surprised, therefore, to find that very early in the poem strange forms and a ruined and haunted Gothic mansion, with spirits and a 'grisly Phantom', are introduced. The mansion reappears with l. 210 and in l. 240 becomes a 'haunted castle' in the process of acquiring a 'pannel'd room' and a richly arrayed female spectre, who conducts the poet to a dungeon. These passages puzzled de Selincourt. Reading them, apparently, simply as Gothic stuff, which of course they are, without local connexion, which they are not, he found it hard to account for the space given them in a poem which Wordsworth himself once described as devoted to his own adventures and the scenery of the region in which he was brought up. Disproportionate they certainly are, but the notebook suggests a reason for them in its references to Calgarth Hall, not the mansion which Bishop Watson built in 1789, but the ancient castellated manor house of the Philipsons near by on the eastern shore of Windermere. It is hardly surprising that a connexion between this place and the haunted mansion of the poem should have escaped latter-day Wordsworthians, for the hall has undergone great changes in the course of its long history. With parts dating from the fourteenth to the seventeenth century, it is today simply a commodious farmhouse. But it was very much more extensive and a very different sort of place in Wordsworth's youth, for West mentions it in his *Guide to the Lakes* as built in the style of Levens Hall and Sizergh Castle,[1] lordly castellated mansions indeed with which the present building could not be compared. It was also ruinous when Wordsworth knew it. West says that it was much out of repair, only partly inhabited, and melancholy in appearance though possessing vestiges of past splendour. *The Beauties of England* speaks of 'half demolished walls . . . overhung with ivy', and of a considerable part as being in ruins.[2] Such a place should obviously be haunted, and so it was. West provides it with many stories of 'frightful visions' and informs us that spectres still were seen. The most notorious of these tales was that of the two skulls which is told in the notebook in two versions on Npp. 13 and 14.

The room on the second floor in the bay window of which the skulls reappeared in spite of all attempts to destroy them, survives to the present day, but the fine panelling with which it was equipped when Christopher and William knew it was removed some years ago. It is obviously the room referred to on Np. 3 as a large one 'cut out in wood with various figures'. I suggest that it is also the 'haunted Castle's pannel'd room' of *The Vale of Esthwaite*, that Calgarth is the 'Gothic mansion' of the poem, that the tales of spectres connected with it suggested the treatment of these elements in the best prevailing Gothic fashion, and that, though they are extended to the point where they are pursued as things in themselves and disrupt the scheme of the whole, it is possible to see their local reference and the way in which they were at least intended to fit into an essentially topographical poem dealing with Esthwaite and such surrounding places as a schoolboy could easily reach. It is quite likely that these things would be perceived without the notebook if we had the proper passages from the topographical writers of the time at hand with the poem. Still, they have not hitherto been perceived.

[1] p. 64.
[2] By Edward Brayley and John Britton (London, 1801–16, 18 vols.), xv. 216–17.

But perception is one thing and evaluation another. Before we attempt the latter, let us examine another point. With l. 270 Wordsworth betakes himself to a

> giddy steep
> That hung loose trembling o'er the deep,

a spot which he tells us that he loved to haunt, and views a lake storm. One of Christopher's entries suggests strongly what he was thinking of. A notation on Np. 9 calls for a description of 'West's 1st station', the first of the several vantage points for viewing Windermere singled out by that writer. It was on the summit of a high crag described as rising 'perpendicularly from the lake' above the peninsula containing the ferry house. Early and late it was also a favourite spot with William Wordsworth. In a Fenwick note to 'Lines Left upon a Seat in a Yew Tree', he alludes to its having been 'long ago pointed out by Mr. West in his Guide' and describes with relish his delight in it while he was a schoolboy. It can hardly be questioned that it is the setting of his very early poem 'Beauty and Moonlight', and it cannot be other than the 'midway cliff' of ll. 89–92 of *An Evening Walk*. Here, then, it would seem, was also the 'giddy steep' of *The Vale of Esthwaite*.

Neither it nor Calgarth is directly mentioned in the poem, nor, aside from the little lake itself and Grasmere, are other places referred to. Much the same is true of *An Evening Walk*. Many years later Wordsworth made a comment on this poem which is largely applicable to both these early descriptive works:

I will conclude my notice of this poem by observing that the plan of it has not been confined to a particular walk or an individual place; a proof (of which I was unconscious at the time) of my unwillingness to submit the poetic spirit to the chains of fact and real circumstance. The country is idealized rather than described in any one of its local aspects.[1]

[1] *Poet. Wks.* i. 319.

What he says is true enough, but, if it is idealization that we have, it is no less true that it is idealization which starts from very specific local reference, a way of working of which Wordsworth made much use in his early poems.

There is another point about his statement worth noting. His remark that he was unconscious during his early career of his unwillingness to submit the poetic spirit to the chains of fact and real circumstance suggests that in his early planning, as distinguished from what happened when he was actually creating, he was quite capable of doing exactly what we find Christopher doing in the notebook—making plans for very specific descriptions. Wordsworth, in short, would appear to have started from such things, and indeed the openly topographical urge in him remained strong throughout his life.

An Evening Walk

It will be clear from what has already been said that *An Evening Walk* was made in part out of the same materials as went into *The Vale of Esthwaite* and that some of its connexions with the notebook are shared with that poem. An instance in point is the plan, on which the whole poem is worked out, of following the times of the day. But in *An Evening Walk* this Miltonic scheme is truncated. After the introductory passages we go directly to a noon-time scene, and succeeding descriptions take us through the afternoon and evening to the dead of night.

The notebook supplies a very likely source of the limiting principle, for a page reference on Np. 5 leads us to the following description of an evening walk in Gray's *Journal to the Lakes* as printed in the Appendix to West's *Guide*:

In the evening I walked alone down to the lake [Derwent Water], by the side of Crow Park, after sunset, and saw the

23

solemn colouring of the night draw on, the last gleam of sunshine fading away on the hill tops, the deep serene of the waters, and the long shadows of the mountains thrown across them, till they nearly touched the hithermost shore. At a distance were heard the murmurs of many waterfalls, not audible in the day time. I wished for the moon, but she was dark to me, and silent,
        Hid in her vacant interlunar cave.[1]

Granted that Wordsworth was quite capable of thinking of an evening walk as the structural principle of a poem without the suggestion of a literary source, and that many such poems had been written in the eighteenth century, still there is one striking couplet of his poem which, with Gray in mind, we cannot fail to notice:

        Ah me! all light is mute amid the gloom,
        The interlunar cavern of the tomb.
                        (ll. 267–8)

It has often been pointed out that this echoes Milton, and it is of course quite possible that it does so directly, but in the light of the notebook entry and the passage in the *Journal* we have good reason to suspect that it came to William, as it came to Christopher, through the medium of the eighteenth-century writer. And if this is true, there can be little question of the influence of that writer's description on the organizing and limiting principle of *An Evening Walk*. We can, in short, relate Wordsworth's practice not merely in a general way to an established tradition but to a specific work in that tradition.

The notebook also leads us to suspect that there was a subsidiary influence, for on Np. 2 we find reference to Dr. Brown's 'Letter'. This was John Brown's *Letter Describing the Vale and Lake of Keswick*, a landmark in the history of the appreciation of Lake district scenery. Written about 1758, it was first published in 1767 at Newcastle and in 1768 in London in Perch's *Collection of Poems by Several Hands*.

[1] p. 206. Cf. Np. 17. Gray quotes *Samson Agonistes*, l. 89.

24

It not only provided a literary model for Gray's *Journal to the Lakes*, which is in the form of a letter to Dr. Wharton, but was the work which sent him to the district in 1769. When, moreover, he took his evening walk to the Lake of Keswick, he was following Brown's specific recommendation of such a nocturnal adventure. Wordsworth, too, can hardly have failed to notice this recommendation. That he knew Brown and knew him early has long been clear from the echo of his 'Rhapsody' pointed out by most editors in ll. 433–4 of *An Evening Walk* and from the praise of Brown in his own *Guide to the Lakes* as one of the discoverers of Lake scenery.[1] His poem, therefore, was the ultimate development of a literary theme which, at least as it applied to the Lake district, had its first expression in Brown and its second in Gray.

An Evening Walk begins with a 'General Sketch of the Lakes'. First we have four lines epitomizing the course of the Derwent, the first brief treatment of a theme, that of tracing the course of a river, which occupied Wordsworth's attention on and off for years and eventually led to the *River Duddon* sonnets. Where did he get this theme? Again we are dealing with a commonplace of topographical writing, but again Christopher's entries direct us to specific materials, for on Np. 17 is a reference to the January 1788 issue of the *European Magazine*. This contains a lengthy review of Gilpin's Lake district *Observations on Picturesque Beauty* with several excerpted passages, one of the most striking of which is an account of the course of the Derwent. There is no good reason to suppose that this was any less in William's background than in Christopher's, for Wordsworth began following this periodical early, a fact proved by his having contributed to it his first published poem, the sonnet 'On Seeing Miss Helen Maria Williams Weep', in February 1787. However much his own experiences may have made the Derwent dear to him and a ready subject for his pen, we

[1] *Prose Wks.* ii. 46–47.

can only conclude that here was a treatment of a theme which he must have seen early and which helped to mould the literary form which his impressions took.[1]

The 'General Sketch' continues with two vignettes which are precisely such as might be expected from a poet who had read the picturesque writers referred to in the notebook. The first gives a 'savage prospect' on Rydal Mere, such a prospect of that little lake as could have been composed only by one whose head was full of Brown's *Letter* with its descriptions of Claude Lorrains in one direction on Derwentwater, Poussins in another, and the shaggy horrors of Salvator Rosa in a third. The four lines on Grasmere which follow, with their directing of the eye to successive features of the scene and their careful enumeration of its components, are also pictorial in manner and suggest nothing so much as the work of an impressionable young man who had read Clarke's analysis of the limitations of Gray's station for viewing the valley and his exposition of the proper constituents of a Grasmere landscape.[2]

The introductory passage is followed by one devoted to establishing the retrospective mood which dominates the poem. This accomplished, the evening walk begins. It really begins, as we have seen, at noon, and a number of lines describe the phenomena of that still time. Schoolboys stretch their length upon the green and round the humming elm, and we are reminded at once of the following entry in the notebook referring to Hawkshead:

[1] It is a further curious fact that William's apostrophe in the sonnet 'To the River Derwent', with its references to a Roman triumph, exactly realizes Christopher's hope to write an apostrophe to the Derwent 'embellished with classical allusions' (L1v.). The sonnet was not published until 1819; its composition is of uncertain date. That it may be very early is suggested by its somewhat tortured syntax.

[2] *Survey of the Lakes* (London, 1789, 2nd ed.), p. 120. Cf. Christopher's references to Clarke's station for viewing Grasmere, which was half way up Butterlip How, on Npp. 10 and 12. In later years the path from Dove Cottage to this point was the favourite walk of William and Dorothy. It is mentioned about once in every twenty pages in her Grasmere *Journal*. William refers to the *Survey* in his note to l. 187 of *An Evening Walk*.

26

> In summer reclined under thy trees or seeking
> thy lake to cool my fervid limbs
>
> (Np. 17)

and of this one:

> [swarms?]
> Summer the ceaseless hum of insects.

In 1794 Wordsworth revised the passage and proposed to substitute among others these lines, which contain in the use of the word 'fervid' another of those extraordinary verbal relationships between the poems and the notebook which have already been pointed out:

> When he who long with languid steps had toiled
> Across the slippery moor, oppressed and foiled
> Sinks down and finds no rest, while as he turns
> The *fervid* earth his languid body burns,
> Nor can his weak arm faintly lifted chase
> The *insect host* that gathers round his face
> And join their murmurs to the tedious sound
> Of seeds of bursting furze that crackle round.
>
> (*Poet. Wks.* i. 8)

The passage did not find a permanent place in the poem.

An Evening Walk proceeds in the 1793 text with a couplet presenting a herd of deer:

> In the brown park, in flocks, the troubl'd deer
> Shook the still twinkling tail and glancing ear.

The deer are in a park because they are those referred to in the following entry:

> G. Park. Deer. Run, then turn &
> gaze at the passenger.

The deer in Gowbarrow Park, a tract of land on Ullswater, and their behaviour at the approach of strangers, made a permanent impression on Wordsworth. He describes them again in his *Guide to the Lakes*,[1] and Dorothy refers to them

---

[1] *Prose Wks.* ii. 115.

twice in the *Journals*.[1] The implications of these facts for Wordsworthian criticism extend beyond the poem; clearly they do not support the frequently advanced notion that it was often Dorothy who perceived and William who echoed. Whatever the relations of Christopher and William may have been, we cannot conclude that the elder brother was following Dorothy simply because a passage in the *Journals* antedates a passage in the poems. We cannot establish even a presumptive case until we have made sure that available information does not reveal materials going back many years. In this instance the notebook suggests exactly such materials, a fact in the light of which many an airy pronouncement upon the literary relations of William and Dorothy becomes suspect.

With l. 125 we come to a curious feature of the poem. The prefatory argument indicates that at this point there was to be a description of a 'Mountain farm, and the Cock'. The cock duly makes his appearance in a mock-heroic passage, but the treatment of the theme of a mountain farm is curiously truncated. It is hard to avoid the conclusion that a subject once intended for development at this point either was left largely untouched or was excised from an earlier version of the poem. It is one that Wordsworth later developed at length in the manner of the very topographical writers who figure so prominently in Christopher's jottings, one to which the younger brother obviously was giving great attention, and with which we can only believe William was also early occupied. The point is of some importance, for it underlies the whole Wordsworthian conception of the Lake district dalesman.[2] Christopher's notations, moreover, since they use the same materials, give us a very good idea of the sort of thing that was apparently once intended for a section in *An Evening Walk*.

The treatment of the theme of village superstitions, intro-

---

[1] i. 132, 421.
[2] See below, pp. 67–71.

duced with l. 175, is illuminated by the notebook in a different way. Wordsworth writes:

> In these lone vales, if aught of faith may claim,
> Thin silver hairs, and ancient hamlet fame;
> When up the hills, as now, retreats the light,
> Strange apparitions mock the village sight.
> A desperate form appears, that spurs his steed,
> Along the midway cliffs with violent speed;
> Unhurt pursues his lengthened flight, while all
> Attend, at every stretch his headlong fall.
> Anon, in order mounts a gorgeous show
> Of horsemen shadows winding to and fro;
> And now the van is gilt with evening's beam
> The rear thro' iron brown betrays a sullen gleam;
> Lost gradual o'er the heights in pomp they go,
> While silent stands th' admiring vale below;
> Till, but the lonely beacon all is fled,
> That tips with eve's last gleam his spiry head.

There are really two themes in these lines, the general one of rural superstitions and the specific one of spectral warriors. Both figure prominently in Christopher's entries and in the writers and works he mentions. To confine our discussion to these, we may notice that the theme of tales told by country folk appears first in Milton's 'L'Allegro' and then in Thomson's *Seasons*, in which we find it at least three times in passages on which Christopher clearly had his eye:

> Mean-time the village rouzes up the fire;
> While well-attested, and as well believ'd,
> Heard solemn, goes the goblin-story round;
> Till superstitious horror creeps o'er all.
> ('Winter', ll. 617–20)
>
> the cottage hind
> Hangs o'er the enlivening blaze, and taleful there
> Recounts his simple frolic; much he talks,
> And much he laughs, nor recks the storm that blows
> Without, and rattles on his humble roof.
> ('Winter', ll. 89–93)

> At fall of Eve the fairy people throng,
> In various game and revelry to pass
> The summer night, as village stories tell.
> ('Summer', ll. 1672–4)

Later in the century Beattie had elaborated the theme in *The Minstrel* (i. xliii–xliv) with its poet who reminded Dorothy so irresistibly of William; and in Collins's 'Ode on the Popular Superstitions of the Highlands of Scotland', first published in 1788, had appeared a whole series of folk tales and beliefs.

In the same manner we can trace in the works referred to in the notebook the notion of spectral armies. Its origin as a literary motif is doubtless to be found in Virgil's description of the portents of disaster which followed the death of Caesar, when 'spectres, pale and wondrous wise, were seen at evening twilight' and 'Germany heard the clash of armies through all the sky' (*Georgics*, i. 474–8). Milton must surely have remembered these lines when he wrote:

> As when to warn proud Cities warr appears
> Wag'd in the troubl'd Skie, and Armies rush
> To Battel in the Clouds.
> (*Paradise Lost*, ii. 533–5)

Thomson attenuates the theme in his worst manner in *The Seasons* ('Autumn', ll. 1113–30), but it also provided him with matter for the superb stanza in *The Castle of Indolence* in which a shepherd of the Hebrides sees at evening a vast assembly of aerial beings moving to and fro (i. 262–70).

It is a plain case of deliberate myth-making when we find this literary theme being attached to specific places and events in English history. The notable instance with which we are directly concerned is the account of spectral warriors on Southerfell which Clarke gives in his *Survey of the Lakes* (pp. 55–56), with which the following entry in the notebook is obviously connected:

> One evening upon Southerfell, there
> were seen armed horse men gallop-
> ing down the hill. etc. enquire of
> this. they were seen twice. Clarke
> mentions them. about 40 years intervened
> between the times. once they appeared
> only as horses, the other time (I believe
> the latter) the year before the rebellion
> as a regt. of soldiers on horseback.
> they thought they heard the breathing, & run
> ing of the horses.
>
> (Np. 14)

We may also conclude from Christopher's entries that he contemplated using either the tale of the Southerfell warriors or that of the Callgarth skulls on Npp. 13–14 in developing the theme of village superstitions.

To return to William's lines on spectral armies, it is reasonable to conclude simply on the basis of a comparison of the two passages that he was following Clarke, as Christopher's entries would lead us to suspect, but in this instance—and the circumstance gives additional support to the method we are following—no debate about the matter is possible, for in a note appended to the lines in the 1793 edition William tells us that he drew from the *Survey*. Christopher's notations, moreover, do more than lead us to an immediate source which is for once verifiable in William's testimony, for they supply a whole thematic background which was as common to the brothers as apparently was Clarke's *Survey* itself.

Comparison of the 1793 text with subsequent revisions shows that Wordsworth's common practice was to reduce or eliminate literary borrowings. But nothing of the sort occurred in the passage on the spectral warriors. On the contrary, it was carefully worked over, and in the final text we have this version:

> The form appears of one that spurs his steed
> Midway along the path with desperate speed;

31

Unhurt pursues his lengthened flight, while all
Attend, at every stretch, his headlong fall.
Anon, appears a brave, a gorgeous show
Of horsemen shadows moving to and fro;
At intervals imperial banners stream,
And now the van reflects the solar beam;
The rear through iron brown betrays a sullen gleam.
While silent stands the admiring crowd below,
Silent the visionary warriors go,
Winding in ordered pomp their upward way,
Till the last banner of their long array
Has disappeared, and every trace is fled
Of Splendour—save the beacon's spiry head
Tipt with eve's latest gleam of burning red.

(ll. 196–211)

The reason for this elaboration is not far to seek. However
they first came to him, stories like that of the Southerfell
horsemen were in time accepted by him as true local legends
—those agencies of power of the significance of which he
tells us both in *The Excursion* (i. 163–9) and the fourth
sonnet of the *Memorials of a Tour in Italy*. The story, as an
'old credulity', a 'tale traditionary round the mountains', was
an object of concern and elaboration because, as we shall
presently see in *The Prelude*, it haunted his imagination for
years.

Among the revisions of *An Evening Walk* presumably
made at Windy Brow in 1794 but not finally incorporated
into the poem, Wordsworth added after the account of the
horsemen an extended passage in which we see again connexions between the poem and notebook. The first of these
comes in the lines

Why shepherds, tremble thus with new alarms
As if ye heard the din of civil arms?

He was clearly still referring to the Southerfell visions and,
it would seem, echoing Clarke's attempt, in the tradition
of Virgil, Milton, and Thomson, to connect the spectral

warriors with presages of civil strife, an attempt of which Christopher's entry also takes note with its reference to the rebellion of 1745. Farther down in the same addition Wordsworth wrote:

> And from the aerial window loves to mark
> The shower o'er road and village driving dark,
> And swains for shelter hurrying from their toil,
> And soon returned to till a freshened soil.

Here it was not Clarke that he had in mind but the *Aeneid*:

> Aeneas, wrathful, stands beneath his shield,
> As when the storm-clouds break in pelting hail,
> And swains and ploughmen from the furrow fly,
> And every traveller cowers in sure defence
> Of river-bank or lofty shelving crag,
> While far and wide it pours; and by and by
> Each, when the sun returns, his task pursues.
> (tr. Williams, x. 802–8)

One of Christopher's entries on Np. 10 echoes the same lines:

> At the beginning of au-
> livid sky in the east. murky clouds
> tumn. day sultry. and overshad
> owed. a [?] unifying haziness.
> a peal of thunder a sudden &
> the torrents descent etc.
> most violent shower lays the
> drives the reaper from his work.
> corn. surprizes the traveller. &
> drives him to seek shelter.

Another connexion between the addition and the notebook —and one in which Christopher leads us to a common source—occurs in the following passage:

> There rent the fen before him and—behold
> A horseman skeleton of giant mould.
> Half-shown erect his mighty bones he rears,
> An unknown being of forgotten years.

Since references in the preceding lines to a beacon suggest

strongly that as Wordsworth wrote he had the region around Penrith in mind (cf. the description of the Penrith beacon in *Prel.* xi. 302–26), there can be little question that the passage was suggested by Clarke's account of the Giant's Grave in the Penrith churchyard and of an occasion on which it was opened and the huge size of its inmate was disclosed. On Np. 12 are some page references scrawled in pencil under later entries in ink alluding to this writer. Investigation shows that they are references to the *Survey*. One of them, that to p. 16, takes us directly to this account.

The episode of the Southerfell horsemen is presently succeeded in *An Evening Walk*, after a passage on the felicity of a family of swans, by the contrasting episode of the forlorn mother. In a note which he appended to this passage in 1794, Wordsworth tells us that it was suggested by an actual incident. There is no good reason to question the reality of this incident and much in what we have seen about his general practice to support it, but we may well question whether it supplies the whole truth about the history of the lines. On this point the notebook does not help us directly, but it does lead us to Knox's *Elegant Extracts of Poetry*, a work which Christopher clearly combed and a worn copy of an early edition of which was included in the sale of William's books at Rydal Mount in 1859. When we thumb through the pages of the Dublin edition of 1789, the one indicated by the references in the notebook, we find the following alleged poem:

A *Winter Piece*

It was a winter's evening, and fast came down the snow,
And keenly o'er the wide heath the bitter blast did blow,
When a damsel all forlorn, quite bewilder'd in her way,
Press'd her baby to her bosom and sadly thus did say:
'Oh! cruel was my father, that shut the door on me,
And cruel was my mother, that such a sight could see;

34

And cruel was the wintry wind, that chills my heart with cold,
And crueller than all, the lad that left my love for gold!
Hush, hush my lovely baby, and warm thee in my breast;
Ah, little thinks thy father how sadly we're distrest!
For cruel as he is, did he know but how we fare,
He'd shield us in his arms from this bitter piercing air.
Cold, cold, my dearest jewel! thy little life is gone:
Oh let my tears revive thee, so warm that trickle down:
My tears that gush so warm, oh they freeze before they fall:
Ah wretched, wretched mother! thou art now bereft of all.'
Then down she sunk despairing upon the drifted snow;
And, wrung with killing anguish, lamented loud her woe:
She kiss'd her baby's pale lips, and laid it by her side;
Then cast her eyes to heaven, then bow'd her head, and died.

(p. 177)

It is quite possible to go through this sorry specimen and
find striking verbal parallels with Wordsworth's lines, but it
is not as a source so much as an analogue that it has significance, for it demonstrates how completely he was working in
the tradition of the eighteenth-century sentimental episode.
A distinction must be made in this case between thematic
origin and concrete materials. He was working in a way
highly characteristic of his early poems—taking a literary
theme, seeking for Lake district counterparts in actual experience, and then refashioning it in accordance with them.

As the poem progresses and night deepens, Wordsworth
thinks of spirits. It was easy enough for him to conceive of
such beings, for before he saw nature as animated by one
great spirit, he peopled it with individual and particular
spirits with independent powers of action.[1] But whatever
degree of credence he may have given them, his handling
of them in *An Evening Walk* was unmistakably moulded by
his reading. The notebook makes this clear about both the
passages dealing with spirits in the latter part of the poem;
and Christopher's jottings, without leading us to any new

[1] *Prel.* i. 351–8 and 490–7; *Recl.,* ll. 33–35.

sources, make it possible to assemble a collocation of materials which gives us a closer view than we have previously had of how well-known literary traditions coalesced to produce what William wrote.

In some lines in *Paradise Lost* Milton had written of angels who at midnight sometimes sang of their Creator from echoing hills.[1] Thomson directly imitated the passage in 'Summer':

> Here, frequent, at the visionary hour,
> When musing midnight reigns on silent noon,
> Angelic harps are in full concert heard,
> And voices chaunting from the wood-crown'd hill,
> The deepening dale, or inmost sylvan glade.
> (ll. 556–60)

But Thomson also gives us much more. Angels are not only heard, but majestic shapes appear who arouse in the poet a 'sacred terror, a severe delight', and who explain that they are spirits who once lived as men. The privilege of hearing the angelic music is bestowed by them alone and only on the contemplative man and on poets.[2]

The guidebook writers of the time, adapting the themes of the poets, also had their say about spirits, particularly in passages describing echoes on the lakes. So much was made of echoes in the latter part of the eighteenth century that all the larger lakes had boats equipped with small brass cannon and horns of various sorts to set echoes off. William Hutchinson in his early *Excursion to the Lakes* describes them at length, remarking on the sevenfold reverberations and the way in which, during the intervals between the apparent dying away of an echo and its renewal, the sound of distant waterfalls was heard.[3] Paying more attention to the echoes of guns than of music, he was yet struck by the fact that the 'music seemed to issue from some resounding temple, which

[1] iv. 680–8.
[3] p. 65. Cf. Npp. 4, 5.
[2] ll. 538–63.

stood concealed behind the mountains', and as the breezes grew softer, he noted that 'one might imagine the voices of a thousand choristers had filled the lengthened chorus'.[1] Later guidebook writers were so impressed by this passage that they frequently reproduced it in full, but Gilpin had his own variations to play on the theme:

But there is another species of ecchoes which are as well adapted to the lake in all its stillness and tranquillity, as the others are to its wildness, and confusion: and which recommend themselves chiefly to those feelings which depend on the greater movements of the mind. Instead of cannon, let a few French horns, and clarionets be introduced. Softer music than such loud wind-instruments, would scarce have power to vibrate. The effect is now wonderfully changed. The sound of the cannon is heard in bursts. It is the modified music of thunder. But the continuation of musical sounds forms a continuation of musical ecchoes; which reverberating around the lake, are exquisitely melodious in their several gradations; and form a thousand symphonies playing together from every part. . . . In short, every rock is vocal, and the whole lake is transformed into a kind of magical scene; in which every promontory seems peopled with aerial beings answering each other in celestial music.

Then Gilpin quotes the lines from Milton at which we have already looked. We observe, however, that in his hands some interesting developments have taken place. For one thing, the effects are now specifically associated with a lake scene. Moreover, Milton's angels are well on the way to becoming, if not fairies, at least beings less specifically Christian. The music indeed seems 'celestial', but the scene is described, not as sacred in its effect, but 'magical'. Clearly, only a small step remained to be taken to associate fairies, genii, and local spirits with it.

We may now look at two passages on fairies in the writers referred to in the notebook. One of them is Thomson's as he

---

[1] pp. 72–73.

tells us of a home-bound swain and milkmaid who wander
into unfrequented regions

> where
> At fall of eve the fairy people throng,
> In various game, and revelry, to pass
> The summer night, as village stories tell.
>   ('Summer', ll. 1671–4)

The other is Beattie's description in *The Minstrel* of fairy
revels at night:

> With merriment, and song, and timbrels clear,
> A troop of dames from myrtle bowers advance;
> The little warriors doff the targe and spear,
> And loud enlivening strains provoke the dance.
> They meet, they dart away, they wheel askance;
> To right, to left, they thrid the flying maze;
> Now bound aloft with vigorous spring, then glance
> Rapid along: with many-coloured rays
> Of tapers, gems, and gold, the echoing forests blaze.

> The dream is fled *etc.*   (I. xxxv–xxxvi)

Now we may notice about Wordsworth and *An Evening
Walk*, first, that he shared the enthusiasm of his contem-
poraries for the echoes of musical instruments. During an
excursion Dorothy and he 'could not but think what a grand
effect the music of the bugle horn would have among these
mountains'.[1] The date of this tour was 1805, but there is no
good reason to think that his feelings about horns were any
different from what they had been in his youth.

There are, to be sure, neither guns nor horns in Wordsworth's poem, but the effects which the guidebook writers
ascribed to them are there and they are developed in terms
of echoes from the passages of the writers at which we have
looked. We have now to see how they were fused, amalga-
mated, and transformed in his imagination. To begin with,
Milton's angels have become simply spirits:

[1] *Prose Wks.* ii. 112.

38

While in sweet cadence rising small and still
The far-off minstrels of the haunted hill,
As the last bleating of the fold expires,
Tune in the mountain dells their water lyres.
(ll. 325–8)

The suggestion of religious feeling is carried over, doubtless from Thomson and Milton in the next lines, but it is not followed up, for Wordsworth was bent on other effects. After a description of deepening night in which 'fairy light' prepares the way, come these lines:

—'Tis restless magic all; at once the bright
Breaks on the shade, the shade upon the light,
Fair Spirits are abroad; in sportive chase
Brushing with lucid wands the water's face,
While music stealing round the glimmering deeps
Charms the tall circle of the enchanted steeps.
—As thro' th' astonished woods the notes ascend,
The mountain streams their rising song suspend;
Below Eve's listening Star the sheep walk stills
It's drowsy tinklings on th' attentive hills;
The milkmaid stops her ballad, and her pail
Stays it's low murmur in th' unbreathing vale;
No night-duck clamours for her wilder'd mate,
Aw'd, while below the Genii hold their state.
—The pomp is fled, and mute the wondrous strains,
No wrack of all the pageant scene remains.
(ll. 345–60)

Here Wordsworth's 'music stealing round the glimmering deeps' makes in Gilpin's language 'every rock . . . vocal' and 'the whole lake is transformed into a kind of magical scene'. As the music ascends, distant waterfalls suspend their song in lines suggestive of Hutchinson's account of the interchange of the echoes of music and the sound of mountain streams. Thomson's milkmaid is there with her pail but without her swain. The abandon of the fairy revel is also reminiscent of Thomson, but when we read in l. 358 that 'the Genii hold their state', and in l. 360 that the 'pageant scene' vanishes, we are entitled to suspect that Beattie was also in mind, and the suspicion deepens to a certainty when we find Wordsworth telling us that 'The pomp is fled' in patent imitation of the formula with which Beattie concludes Edwin's vision.

The poem comes to end with what is in effect a more or less formal 'night piece'. Poems and parts of poems of this sort, of course, are of frequent occurrence among the eighteenth-century poets. Such pieces invited localization and adaptation to the purposes of Lake district description. The vogue was set by Dr. John Brown, the first real connoisseur of Lake scenery, who composed about the middle of the century as a poetic addition to his prose *Letter describing the Vale and Lake of Keswick* a verse 'Rhapsody, Written at the Lakes in Westmorland'. All that survives of the poem are the following lines, which Wordsworth later quoted in his own *Guide to the Lakes*:

> Now sunk the sun, now twilight sunk, and night
> Rode in her zenith; not a passing breeze
> Sigh'd to the grove, which in the midnight air
> Stood motionless, and in the peaceful floods
> Inverted hung: for now the billow slept
> Along the shore, now heav'd the deep, but spread
> A shining mirror to the moon's pale orb,
> Which dim and waining, o'er the shadowy cliffs
> The solemn woods, and spiry mountain tops,
> Her glimmering faintness threw: now every eye,
> Oppress'd with toil, was drown'd in deep repose;
> Save that the unseen shepherd in his watch,
> Prop'd by his crook, stood listening by the fold,
> And gaz'd the starry vault and pendant moon;
> Nor voice, nor sound, broke on the deep serene,
> But the soft murmur of swift-gushing rills,
> Forth issuing from the mountain's distant steep,
> (Unheard till now, and now scarce heard) proclaim'd
> All things at rest, and imag'd the still voice
> Of quiet whispering in the ear of night.

These lines were printed in Richard Cumberland's *Odes* in 1776 and thereafter had wide circulation. They established once and for all that a Keswick night scene, complete with the light of the moon and the sound of waterfalls unheard by day but audible in the stillness of the night, was expected from a Lake writer. Gray, who read Brown's encomium and took off for the Lakes, reached the high point of his *Journal* in developing the theme in a passage which we have already had occasion to notice, and the guidebook writers followed as best they could in unashamed imitation.

Christopher's notations take us back to all these things and give ample evidence of his intention to attempt a Keswick night piece. The last entry on Np. 1 calls for a description of a sail 'on Derwent by night', and on Np. 17 we find this unlocalized entry:

> I have often watched the sun setting, & the last beam
> upon the eastern hills, & the slow shades of night
> invest the pole. The Moon.
> The expiring song. cuckow etc the last
> red fade in the west & sober grey
> succeed. the watch dog. the owl. or the
> voice sounding accross the lake.

This notation is in the manner of both Brown's lines and William's concluding ones. If it has no other value, it and the citations which underlie it suggest that it is not enough to point out casual parallels between Gray and Brown and the final passage of *An Evening Walk* as scholars have long been doing. If we would have a more exact understanding of the mode in which Wordsworth was working, we must realize that he was not merely indulging in variations on a common theme of topographical poetry but adapting a special variety of it which flourished among Lake writers.

The adaptation, however, turns out to be something more than just a Keswick night piece. It is in fact not localized at all, and the sound images connected with the allusion to

41

the ferryman suggest not Derwentwater but Windermere. The processes involved were those of idealization and fusion. The passage is the best illustration in the entire poem of that idealization which its author claimed for it as a whole. Here he was doing much more than casting the description of local scenes into literary moulds and then depriving them of their identity. In these lines we see the imagination at work in the Coleridgean sense—the coadunating, secondary, poetic imagination which first breaks down and then creates anew through those processes of amalgamation and fusion which Professor Lowes some years ago studied so brilliantly in Coleridge himself. It is for this reason that the passage is the finest that Wordsworth had written or that he was to write for some time. It is one of the great manipulations of the images of sound in his poetry.

Descriptive Sketches

The Fenwick note on *Descriptive Sketches* tells us that it was composed in 1791–2. Along with *An Evening Walk*, it was 'huddled up' for publication at the beginning of 1793. The two poems are closely related, for though there is much in *Descriptive Sketches* which derives from local circumstance and primitivistic notions about the Swiss common at the time, we also see and hear in it sights and sounds of the Lake district adapted to continental settings. It would not be surprising, therefore, were we to find connexions between it and the materials of the notebook.

The most striking of these appears in the lines describing a chamois-hunter who perishes in a snow-storm:

> At once bewildering mists around him close
> And cold and hunger are his least of woes;
> The Demon of the snow with angry roar
> Descending, shuts for aye his prison door.

Craz'd by the strength of hope at morn he eyes
As sent from heaven the raven of the skies,
Then with despair's whole weight his spirits sink,
No bread to feed him, and the snow his drink,
While ere his eyes can close upon the day,
The eagle of the Alps o'ershades his prey.
    Meanwhile his wife and child with cruel hope
All night the door at every moment ope;
Haply that child in fearful doubt may gaze,
Passing his father's bones in future days,
Start at the relics of that very thigh,
On which so oft he prattled when a boy.

(ll. 398–413)

The notebook contains on L3r. a reference to Thomson's
Seasons, p. 175, and on L1v. we also find p. 356 of Knox's
Elegant Extracts cited. When we follow these leads, we
come to the following lines, which are clearly the basis of
an entry on Np. 18 calling for a 'Description of a man perishing in the snow'; in fact, the lines are printed in *Elegant
Extracts* under that title:

As thus the snows arise; and foul, and fierce,
All Winter drives along the darken'd air:
In his own loose revolving fields, the swain
Disaster'd stands; sees other hills ascend
Of unknown joyless brow; and other scenes,
Of horrid prospect, shag the trackless plain:
Nor finds the river, nor the forest hid
Beneath the formless wild; but wanders on
From hill to dale, still more and more astray

. . . .

While round him night resistless closes fast,
And every tempest, howling o'er his head,
Renders the savage wilderness more wild

. . . .

              down he sinks
Beneath the shelter of the shapeless drift.
Thinking o'er all the bitterness of death,

Mix'd with the tender anguish Nature shoots
Thro' the wrung bosom of the dying Man,
His wife, his children, and his friends unseen.
In vain for him the officious wife prepares
The fire fair-blazing, and the vestment warm;
In vain his little children, peeping out
Into the mingling storm, demand their sire,
With tears of artless innocence. Alas!
Nor wife, nor children, more shall he behold,
Nor friends, nor sacred home. On every nerve
The deadly Winter seizes; shuts up sense;
And, o'er his inmost vitals creeping cold,
Lays him among the snows, a stiffened corse,
Stretch'd out, and bleaching in the northern blast.
                    ('Winter', ll. 276–321)

Clearly, Thomson gives us the theme; Christopher's entries
contemplate its localization in the Lake district; and William in *Descriptive Sketches*, in a passage which is still arti-
ficial enough, but in concision and imaginative realization
a vast improvement on Thomson's over-lengthy elaboration, carries it over to a Swiss setting, providing a thematic
counterpart to the catastrophe of the poor woman who, at
least in the 1794 revisions of *An Evening Walk*, perishes
with her babes in a snow-storm.

But if Wordsworth wrote with echoes of Thomson in
mind, the notebook also leads us to some other lines in which
a bewildered person meets disaster. In his 'Ode on the
Popular Superstitions of the Highlands of Scotland', Collins
describes the night spirits and monsters of bogs which mis-
lead travellers with false lights at night. The monsters who
are imagined by the shepherd in the evening mist in Christopher's second entry on Np. 7 undoubtedly reflect this
passage. That it also underlies William's lines is suggested
by the fact that whereas in Thomson the wife busily prepares for her husband's return and the children whimper at
the tardiness of their sire, the alarm of the waiting wife is

stressed in the 'Ode' as it is in *Descriptive Sketches*. The Collins influence appears too in Wordsworth's reference to the storm as caused by the 'Demon of the snow', and in the revisions which he made in 1794 the anxious wife goes to the gate to meet the unlucky man as the children do in Collins's poem. It has indeed long been known that Collins was one of the poets that Wordsworth read early. But the connexions suggested by Christopher's entries cast a fuller light on the 'Remembrance of Collins' which William had written in 1789 and make more specific the significance of his admiration for that poet.

Some lines farther on in *Descriptive Sketches* we come to a passage on a morning scene in which a valley filled with mist is viewed from a superior height:

> 'Tis morn: with gold the verdant mountain glows,
> More high, the snowy peaks with hues of rose.
> Far stretch'd beneath the many-tinted hills,
> A mighty *waste* of mist the valley fills,
> A solemn sea! whose vales and mountains round
> Stand motionless, to awful silence bound.
> A *gulf* of gloomy view, that opens wide
> And bottomless, divides the midway tide.
> Like leaning masts of stranded ships appear
> The pines that near the coast their summits rear
> Of cabins, woods, and lawns a pleasant shore
> Bounds calm and clear the chaos still and hoar:
> Loud thro' that midway gulf ascending, sound
> Unnumber'd streams with hollow roar profound.
> Mounts thro' the nearer mist the chaunt of birds,
> And talking voices, and the low of herds,
> The bark of dogs, the drowsy tinkling bell,
> The wild-wood mountain lutes of saddest swell.
> Think not, suspended from the *cliff* on high
> He looks below with undelighted eye.
>
> (ll. 492–511)

De Selincourt pointed out that this passage owes not a little to a stanza in Beattie's *The Minstrel*, a poem peculiarly associated with Wordsworth's early career:

> And oft the craggy *cliff* he loved to climb,
> When all in mist the world below was lost.
> What dreadful pleasure! there to stand sublime,
> Like shipwrecked mariner on desert coast,
> And view the enormous *waste* of vapour, tossed
> In billows lengthening to the horizon round,
> Now scooped in *gulfs*, with mountains now embossed!
> And hear the voice of mirth and song rebound,
> Flocks, herds, and waterfalls, along the hoar profound.
>
> (I. xxi)

Simply on the evidence of the lines alone, surely most readers will hardly question the conclusion that here is the real thematic origin of Wordsworth's lines.

Now when we turn to the notebook, we find that *The Minstrel* is three times referred to,[1] and in the two notations in which it is mentioned by name it is associated with the theme of mists. Another entry begins: 'Morning. Mist. (not the elaborate description)'. Certainly we may at least suspect that what Christopher intended as the 'elaborate description' was a passage based on Beattie's stanza, exactly such a description as we find realized in *Descriptive Sketches*.

But this is not all we find. The notebook also, as we have seen, contains references to Clarke's *Survey of the Lakes*, a work to which William refers in a note to *An Evening Walk*. Clarke, too, was one of those topographical writers who went to the poets to tell them what to look for in scenery, and before Wordsworth went to Beattie, Clarke had been there. The evidence is an elaborate passage:

I am pleased with an evening walk as well as Dr. Brown or Mr. Gray; yet I had rather be up at four o'clock in a calm morning, and walk about half way up Skiddow, if there is a fog or mist in the valley: for when the mist lyes in the valleys very thick

---

[1] Np. 4 and L1r. See also p. 283 of *Elegant Extracts*, cited on L1v.

46

in a morning, the tops of the mountains are quite clear. This is very curious, and no traveller has been acquainted with it, except one, who says thus of it:

[Quotes Beattie's stanza]

About half way up the mountain, or not quite so high, you will be above the mist, which lyes thick and white below. It is quite level and appears so strong that you might walk upon it; I can compare it to nothing so much as to a vast sheet of ice covered with snow; not a house or a tree can be seen; the voice of extremely distant waterfalls is heard perfectly distinct, and not one confusing another. The loud crowing cock at every village, joined to the warbling of the smaller-feathered choir, comes with an almost magical sweetness to the ear, whilst the bellowing bulls and cows form a rural base to the concert; every sound is much more distinctly heard than at any other time. The words of men conversing at two miles distance are perfectly intelligible; the whistling of the shepherd going to his fleecy care seems close to you, though he cannot be seen. Nor is the eye less delighted, for the tops of distant mountains are now as distinctly viewed with the naked eye, as at other times with the help of a telescope: but these pleasures are of short duration, for as soon as the rising sun gets a little power, the mists quickly disperse, and the objects relapse into their ordinary state.

(pp. 72–73)

This elaboration, preposterous as it is in diction, was Clarke's principal contribution to the stock of Lake district descriptive themes. After the appearance of the *Survey* the guide-book writers, who borrowed from one another with reckless abandon, took it over from him along with Beattie's stanza. In a book from which by his own evidence he had earlier drawn, William cannot have missed it. That he did not miss it and that echoes from it fused in his mind with those from Beattie is strongly suggested also by the circumstance that some of the sound images in his lines, notably those referring to the songs of birds and the voices of talking men, occur in Clarke's account but not in Beattie's poem. Moreover, the 'shepherd going to his fleecy care' in the *Survey*

47

provides the setting in which the whole description is placed in Wordsworth's lines.

Guilt and Sorrow

The Prelude aside, nothing that Wordsworth ever wrote cost him more trouble or was the subject of more extended revision than the powerful and unpleasant poem *Guilt and Sorrow*. Two points about its history are important in estimating its relation to entries in the notebook. One is that though the so-called first version is usually assigned to 1793–4, Wordsworth says in the Fenwick note that much of the 'Female Vagrant's story' was composed at least two years before. Strong reasons for accepting this statement are found in a fragment which is clearly related to this tale and which de Selincourt persuasively assigns to 1791. In the second place, in reworking the poem, Wordsworth early and late was concerned about the problem of its unity. He was bothered, in short, by the same thing that disturbed him in his notorious note about *The Ancient Mariner*—the adequacy of the extent to which the incidents produced one another. In attempting to solve this problem he handled materials with easy freedom. In one version the cottage of the Vagrant's father is by 'Derwent's side'; in another it is at Taunton Dean, 'far distant in the west'. In 1799, when he contemplated supplying her with a new story, he considered making her a widow or sister or daughter of the man murdered by the Sailor. Such changes, of course, are the poet's prerogative. I mention them here simply to point out that he availed himself of it freely.

The part of the poem which concerns us most is the first part of the tale of the Female Vagrant. For the first twenty years of her life, we are told in the late final version, she had lived in rustic quiet and happiness with her parents on the little piece of land they owned. Then misfortune overtook them and finally, the mother having died, her father was dis-

48

possessed of his 'old hereditary nook' and they were forced to leave. Alternative versions in the early revisions give us additional details about their difficulties. It appears from the version of 1793–4 that they were victims of 'Oppression', and that the father's 'little range of water' was denied. Obviously a villain was at work; and in the version which appeared as 'The Female Vagrant' in the *Lyrical Ballads* of 1798, he emerges into the open as a rapacious landowner who built 'a mansion proud our woods among', brought cottage after cottage under his sway, and took no joy in seeing fields that he did not possess. The Vagrant's father refused the gold proffered for his little farm, and this, we are told, was the beginning of all his troubles. He became the victim of injury after injury and finally his all was seized except the bed on which he lay.

The fragment of 1791 which is associated with this poem contains two stanzas in which a wretched woman begins to tell her story. It starts out very much like the tale of the Female Vagrant, only now the narrator is not a daughter but the wife or widow of the owner of the little farm.

When we put all these facts together, it seems not unreasonable to believe that the story of the Calgarth skulls, told in the notebook in two versions on Npp. 13–14, and as available to William as it was to Christopher, may have suggested the first part of the Female Vagrant's story, and the likelihood is increased by the heavy drawing on Calgarth lore which we have already observed in *The Vale of Esthwaite*. Common elements are the rich landowner, the desired piece of land on a lake, the cottager who refuses to sell, and, in the second version of the tale as told in the notebook, legal chicanery resulting in his complete ruin. These elements were the residual, usable parts of a story so fantastic in some respects that it excited the ridicule even of the topographical writers. William could use them because they were supposed to have happened in places he knew and therefore supplied that basis for literary themes in actual experience of which he was ever in quest. For there can be no question of the literary theme. It is that of the cottager wrongly dispossessed by the great landowner which was one of the prime preoccupations of eighteenth-century sentimentalism. Nor do we need to look far to find it in Wordsworth's immediate literary background, for Goldsmith had written in *The Deserted Village*, a poem which echoes in *An Evening Walk*, as editors have often pointed out:

> Amid thy bowers the tyrant's hand is seen,
> And desolation saddens all the green:
> One only master grasps the whole domain,
> And half a tillage stints thy smiling plain.
>
> (ll. 37–40)

It is the notebook which leads us, for the first time so far as I am aware, to the local materials in terms of which Wordsworth developed this theme. And these materials were important to him. They appealed to that strong sense of fact which he considered an essential basis of his poetry and which led him again and again in notes to his poems to cite an actual incident as the basis of them even when he was developing conventional themes of the time.

The Borderers

Only one incident in *The Borderers* appears to be related to the notebook. In Act II, scene ii, in which the villainous Oswald tells Marmaduke his story, we learn of the crime which became the motivating obsession of his life—the abandoning on a desert island of a ship captain whom he believed to have dealt treacherously with him. The place was a bare rock without food, water, grass, or shade.

Here we have one of those crimes of alienation which, like the sins of Peter Bell and the Ancient Mariner, occupied so much of Wordsworth's and Coleridge's attention during the days when the *Lyrical Ballads* were taking shape. It is also,

50

like the Mariner's violation of the principle of the 'one life', a crime of alienation committed at sea. Had Wordsworth not found use for it in *The Borderers*, this rather than the shooting of an albatross, which he claimed to have suggested to Coleridge, might have provided the theme for the initial collaborative endeavour out of which *The Ancient Mariner* grew. It might have been Wordsworth who took over the poem, rather than Coleridge, and *Peter Bell* might never have been written.

What was in Wordsworth's mind as he fashioned Oswald's story? One of Christopher's entries suggests a likely answer, for on L1*v.* we find reference to p. 489 of Knox's *Elegant Extracts of Poetry*. When we turn to this page, we find under the title 'Description of a Person Left on a Desert Island' Melisander's account of how through the treachery of Egisthus he was abandoned on an island and left to die:

> - - - - - - - - - -Next night—a dreary night!
> Cast on the wildest of the Cyclad Isles,
> Where never human foot had marked the shore,
> These ruffians left me.- - - - - - - - - - - - - - -
> - - - - - - - - - - - - - - - - Beneath a shade
> I sat me down, more heavily oppress'd
> More desolate at heart, than e'er I felt
> Before. When Philomela o'er my head
> Began to tune her melancholy strain,
> As piteous of my woes; till, by degrees,
> Composing sleep on wounded nature shed
> A kind but short relief. At early morn,
> Wak'd by the chaunt of birds, I look'd around
> For usual objects: objects found I none,
> Except before me stretched the toiling main,
> And rocks and woods, in savage view, behind.
> (Agamemnon, III. i)

However much the details may vary, again we find a basic thematic similarity between Christopher's entries and William's poems. Moreover, the idea of abandonment is central not only to one episode in *The Borderers* but to the entire action of the play, for it becomes the crime of Marmaduke and Eldred as well as of Oswald, a point explicitly brought out in the recognition when Marmaduke exclaims on hearing Eldred's confession:

> Oh Monster! Monster! there are three of us,
> And we shall howl together.
>
> (v. 2059–60)

The Prelude

One is scarcely well into *The Prelude* before one relationship with the notebook becomes apparent. We read of bird-snaring at night and in the autumn, of robbing ravens' nests in the daytime and the spring, of boating on Ullswater in the evening and the summer, of ice-skating on Esthwaite on winter evenings, and of indoor sports on winter nights. Clearly there is no exact distribution of these incidents on the Miltonic scheme of following the times of the day on which Christopher had planned to draw so heavily and which William also used frequently in his juvenilia; yet just as clearly traces of the influence of that scheme are still discernible. Moreover, fused with the vestiges of this Miltonic plan are evidences of a loose seasonable distribution of the incidents in the manner of Thomson, the same sort of fusion which Christopher's notations show. This method of proceeding, moreover, is carried over into Book II, Wordsworth himself summing up the point for us in some lines which make it explicit:

> 'Twere long to tell
> What spring and summer, what the winter snows,
> And what the summer shade, what day and night,
> The evening and the morning, what my dreams
> And what my waking thoughts supplied, to nurse
> The spirit of religious love in which
> I walked with Nature. (ii. 371–7)

One gathers that several interwoven principles of arrangement govern the disposition of the incidents in the opening books of the poem. At the same time that Wordsworth was tracing his development he also carried over schemata from his early descriptive plans.

When we come to specific incidents, our attention rests first on the account of skating on Esthwaite. There is nothing in the poem that springs more directly out of his own experience. But this docs not alter the fact, to which the notebook directs our attention, that ice-skating was a theme of eighteenth-century descriptive poetry and that the citation of 'Addison's Latine Poem' on Np. 17 offers us a treatment of this theme which was very probably in William's background as well as Christopher's. This must have been the pseudo-Addisonian 'Cursus Glacialis', a poem asserted to be Addison's in Curll's edition of 1725, but given to Philip Frowde in *Musae Anglicanae.* This supplied the literary theme, but it was one which apparently fired Christopher's imagination as well as William's, for even in the notebook entry it has already been completely personalized and it would seem that an autobiographical treatment was intended, perhaps as an interlude in the descriptive poem which he had in mind. Here the younger brother's entry affords a parallel to the process by which I would suggest that William also worked. There is little enough of the literary model remaining in Christopher's entry, and scarcely more in William's lines in *The Prelude.* The passage forms one of the most striking illustrations of the way in which Wordsworth revitalized old themes by pouring into them his own experience. He did, of course, something more. His poetry appeared new and significant to perceptive readers in his own time not because of any absolute novelty of theme and not even wholly because he infused into it fresh and original materials, but because he invested commonplace descriptive themes with deeper and more profound experience and drew from it implications which he used in the complicated philosophical edifice he erected.

A similar relationship between poem and notebook, again with an eighteenth-century model, exists in the account of the robbing of ravens' nests in Book I. An entry on Np. 2 is concerned with the robbing of an eagle's nest as a poetic theme and gives a reference to Gray's account of the exploit of a Borrowdale farmer in the *Journal to the Lakes*. Bird passages are a recurrent theme of descriptive poetry, at least from Thomson on, and if we can judge from such works as Budworth's *Windermere, a Poem* (1798), there is evidence that Gray's account established the robbing of an eagle's nest as a proper motif for Lake description. Wordsworth's account is the thematic equivalent of Gray's. Here again it would look as if a theme of eighteenth-century description had been taken over, individualized in terms of the poet's own experience, and adapted to the purposes of autobiographical poetry. In this case the process would appear to have been so complete that resemblance in detail between the original descriptive model and the ultimate poetic result fades out completely. Again, however, we observe the attaching of profound personal significances to an episode which in the hands of other writers was only a cause of local triumph and rejoicing in a Lake district vale.

A somewhat different process and one which raises important questions is observable in some lines which Wordsworth ultimately rejected. Christopher's fascination with the tale of the spectral horsemen of Southerfell was shared by William, for we have already seen him using it in *An Evening Walk*. The story lingered in Wordsworth's mind. I believe it has not previously been pointed out that in some lines which De Selincourt prints in his Notes the spectral procession again makes its way:

> when in my bed I lay
> Alone in darkness, I have seen the gloom
> Peopled with shapes, arrayed in hues more bright

Than flowers or gems, or than *the evening sky;*
Processions, multitudes in wake or fair
Assembled, puppet shows with *trum[p]et, fife,*
Wild beasts, and *standards* waving in the [field?]
These mounting ever in a sloping line
Were followed by the tumult of the shew
Of *horses* [?   ]
These *vanishing,* appeared another scene—
Hounds, and the uproar of the ch[ace], or *steeds*
That galloped like the wind through standing corn.
Then came a thron[g] of forms all [?   ]
Then headless trunks and faces horrible,
Unutterably, horribly arranged
In parallel lines, in feature and in look
All different, yet marvelously akin;
Then *files of soldiery* with *dazzling arms*
Still *mounting, mounting upwards,* each to each
Of all these *spectres* every band and cl[ass?]
Succeeding with fa[n]tastic difference
And instant unimaginable change.

(*Prel.*, pp. 521–2)

There can be no doubt of the phenomenon if the words I
have italicized are read in sequence. And the phenomenon,
as we have discovered, was based on a story told in Clarke's
Survey. We might therefore think that once, at least, Wordsworth went so far as to represent as an actual occurrence
what was only literary in origin. We might even conclude
that the final exclusion of the lines from the poem was due
to a certain sense of spuriousness about them. But such
notions would certainly be erroneous. The vision of Druids
on Salisbury Plain in Book XII (ll. 312–54) suggests the
proper explanation. In this well-known passage, however he
conceived the mind as operating on sensation, there was
clearly an externalization of mental images based on his
reading—something akin, at least, to what Coleridge called
'ocular spectra'. Such appearances Coleridge associated with
states of anxiety, excitement, and the hovering between

waking and sleeping, when the mind took a hint from something external and added to it, 'through Tom Wedgewood's ground principle of the influx of memory on perception', materials which produced a distinct vision.[1] Such experiences were real for Coleridge, and both the lines on the Druids and those on the spectral warriors show that they were real for Wordsworth.

Another notable relationship between notebook and poem emerges when we examine the long and carefully written entry on Np. 8. Though it is Christopher's, there is much about it simply as it stands which suggests William. One thing is the complaint of the treachery of memory. Though he may be said to have founded *The Prelude* on memory and complaints of its treachery were a convention of the age, there can be no question that he had a keen sense of its limitations.[2] The lines, too, are Wordsworthian in manner, for though assuredly we do not have the language of the common people purified, we do have the sort of expanded simile in the Miltonic tradition in which Wordsworth at times indulged. But what is most characteristic about the entry, of course, is its references to 'spots' in the writer's memory which are clearer than others, which have a special significance for him, and upon which he dwells. Inevitably, we are led to compare the entry with the justly celebrated lines in *The Prelude*:

> There are in our existence spots of time
> That with distinct pre-eminence retain
> A vivifying Virtue, whence, depress'd
> By false opinion and contentious thought,
> Or aught of heavier or more deadly weight,

---

[1] *Anima Poetae*, ed. E. H. Coleridge (London, 1895), pp. 91 and 45; *Letters*, ed. E. H. Coleridge (London, 1892, 2 vols.), i. 341 and 427–8; and *Miscellaneous Criticism*, ed. T. M. Raysor (London, 1936), p. 388. See also Dougald M. Monroe's unpublished Northwestern University dissertation 'Coleridge's Theories of Dreams, Hallucinations, and Related Phenomena' (1953), pp. 110–46.

[2] *Prel.* xi. 334–43; the Fenwick note to *The Borderers*; *E.L.*, pp. 34–35.

In trivial occupations, and the round
Of ordinary intercourse, our minds
Are nourish'd and invisibly repair'd,
A virtue by which pleasure is enhanced
That penetrates, enables us to mount
When high, more high, and lifts us up when fallen.
This efficacious spirit chiefly lurks
Among those passages of life in which
We have the deepest feeling that the mind
Is lord and master, and that outward sense
Is but the obedient servant of her will.
Such moments, worthy of all gratitude,
Are scatter'd everywhere, taking their date
From our first childhood: in our childhood even
Perhaps are most conspicuous. Life with me,
As far as memory can look back, is full
Of this beneficent influence.   (xi. 258–79)

What are we to conclude when this passage is placed side
by side with Christopher's entry? Not certainly that the two
had the same conception of spots of time and not that William
was drawing from Christopher's notes or that Christopher
drew from his, though one or the other may have done
so. The significance of the entry lies in the fact that it
presents the central concept of the special significance in
the memory of certain key experiences in a form which
stands midway between conventional eighteenth-century
variations on the theme that we remember some things
better and with more delight than others, an idea rooted in
the association psychology, and the idea, invested with
relevances to Wordsworth's transcendentalized theory of
knowledge and his conception of God and immortality,
which we find in *The Prelude*. The thematic origin in the
previous age, in short, emerges once more in concepts which
are at the heart of his experience, and affords another striking
proof that the Wordsworthian synthesis was made out
of materials at hand and often conventional.

In examining *Descriptive Sketches* we discovered a

passage dealing with mist in a valley as viewed from a superior eminence and found it to be an elaboration and adaptation to a Swiss setting of a theme which had appeared in Beattie's *The Minstrel* and which is pointed to by an entry in the notebook. At the opening of Book XIII of *The Prelude* we find an account of the climbing of Snowdon in Wales to see the sunrise. When he was part-way up the mountain, Wordsworth tells us

> The Moon stood naked in the Heavens, at height
> Immense above my head, and on the shore
> I found myself of a huge sea of mist,
> Which, meek and silent, rested at my feet:
> A hundred hills their dusky backs upheaved
> All over this still Ocean, and beyond,
> Far, far beyond, the vapours shot themselves,
> In headlands, tongues, and promontory shapes,
> Into the Sea, the real Sea, that seem'd
> To dwindle and give up its majesty,
> Usurp'd upon as far as sight could reach.
> Meanwhile, the Moon looked down upon this shew
> In single glory, and we stood, the mist
> Touching our very feet; and from the shore
> At distance not the third part of a mile
> Was a blue chasm; a fracture in the vapour,
> A deep and gloomy breathing place through which
> Mounted the roar of waters, torrents, streams
> Innumerable, roaring with one voice.
> The universal spectacle throughout
> Was shaped for admiration and delight,
> Grand in itself alone, but in that breach
> Through which the homeless voice of waters rose,
> The dark deep thoroughfare had Nature lodg'd
> The Soul, the Imagination of the whole.
>
> (ll. 41–65)

The lines are weighted with philosophical implications and are several different things at once; among these it is clear that they are another variation on the descriptive theme of

58

mist in a valley seen from above which had first attracted Wordsworth's attention in his youth. Some of the most notable passages of his great creative period developed, in short, out of his early descriptive interests.

One that did not ultimately find its way into *The Prelude*, but that was once clearly intended for it, is brought to light when we observe that a number of Christopher's notations show a marked interest in the theme of the destructive autumn storm with floods and whirlwinds which came down from the First Books of *The Georgics* and of Lucretius and had been developed by Thomson in some passages noted by page references to his works on L1r. It is obvious, too, that the interest which the entries on Npp. 1 and 4 display in the Legberthwaite or St. John's storm of 1749 provided analogous Lake district materials for the development of the theme. But a notation on Np. 16 also shows us that a storm which occurred in 1790 in the Coniston region competed with the older one in supplying local detail. Now a St. John's storm does not appear in *The Prelude*, nor indeed does a Coniston one, but MS. W contains the following lines:

> It was a day
> Upon the edge of Autumn, fierce with storm;
> The wind blew through the hills of Coniston
> Compress'd as in a tunnel; from the lake
> Bodies of foam took flight, and the whole vale
> Was wrought into commotion high and low—
> Mist flying up and down, bewilder'd showers,
> Ten thousand thousand waves, mountains and crags,
> And darkness, and the sun's tumultuous light.
> Green leaves were rent in handfulls from the trees,
> The mountains all seem'd silent, din so near
> Peal'd in the traveller's ear, the clouds [?]
> The horse and rider staggered in the blast,
> And he who looked upon the stormy lake
> Had fear for boat or vessel where none was.
>
> *(Prel.*, p. 601)

59

However individualized these lines may be, they are yet the thematic counterpart of the storms referred to in the notebook, and the notebook, moreover, would appear to suggest why the unlocalized storms of literary tradition came to be associated in Wordsworth's lines specifically with Coniston.

There is one more major thematic relationship between the notebook and *The Prelude*. On Np. 11 Christopher records a plan to 'introduce an Hymn in imitation of Milton's and Thompson's'. The reference is clearly to *Paradise Lost*, v, 153–208, the morning hymn of Adam and Eve in the Garden before the Fall, and to the 'Hymn to the Seasons'. It is common to both these hymns that all created things join to praise God and that the question is asked whether man alone is not to join in the universal diapason. In an entry on Np. 18 this theme is worked into a passage describing sensations in the Esthwaite region:

> I have joined
> my voice to that of the birds, flocks etc.
> to thank my Maker
> say shall not man pour out the
> song of gratitude when he knows
> the source from whence all these
> blessings arise to their author.

When we turn from Christopher to William we find, first, that in a letter from the Continent to Dorothy in the autumn of 1790, he tells her that in the Alps he had 'not a thought of man, or a single created being', and that his 'whole soul was turned to him who produced the terrible majesty' before him.[1] Here indeed Milton's and Thomson's hymns hardly express his feeling; he writes, in fact, almost as if he had them in mind and found that what they described was not what he experienced. None the less, there can be no question of their influence on him. The evidence is found in the hymn

[1] *E.L.*, p. 33.

60

of the Wanderer near the beginning of the Fourth Book of
The Excursion:

> How beautiful this dome of sky;
> And the vast hills, in fluctuation fixed
> At thy command, how awful! Shall the Soul,
> Human and rational, report of thee
> Even less than these! Be mute who will, who can,
> Yet I will praise thee with impassioned voice.
>
> (ll. 34–39)

Moreover, it is found in one of the memorable passages of
The Prelude:

> I was only then
> Contented when with bliss ineffable
> I felt the sentiment of Being spread
> O'er all that moves, and all that seemeth still,
> O'er all, that, lost beyond the reach of thought
> And human knowledge, to the human eye
> Invisible, yet liveth to the heart,
> O'er all that leaps, and runs, and shouts, and sings,
> Or beats the gladsome air, o'er all that glides
> Beneath the wave, yea, in the wave itself
> And mighty depth of waters. Wonder not
> If such my transports were; for in all things now
> I saw one life, and felt that it was joy.
> One song they sang, and it was audible,
> Most audible then when the fleshly ear,
> O'ercome by grosser prelude of that strain,
> Forgot its functions, and slept undisturb'd.
>
> (ii. 418–34)

Moreover, with some shifting, no doubt, of Wordsworth's
views, in the 1850 text the universal song in which man par-
ticipates becomes explicitly one of adoration as all things
look toward the Uncreated, and the resemblance to Milton's
and Thomson's lines is heightened:

> Wonder not
> If high the transport, great the joy I felt,
> Communing in this sort through earth and heaven

61

With every form of creature, as it looked
Towards the Uncreated with a countenance
Of adoration, with an eye of love.
One song they sang *etc.*

(ii. 409–15)

If we take the letter of 1790, the passage in *The Prelude* of
1805–6, and that in the 1850 version as representing three
stages in Wordsworth's development, the evidence suggests
that he early reacted against the hymns of Milton and
Thomson because they could not meet the rigorous test of
accordance with his own experience which he habitually
imposed on literary themes; that later their formulas became congenial to him because they were adaptable to the
faith in the 'one life' which characterized him at the high
tide of his powers; and that at a still later time, as power
and certainty both faded from him, he fell back more and
more on the conceptions of the poets who had attracted his
attention in his youth.

Several lesser connexions of various sort exist between the
notebook and *The Prelude*. The most important of these is
Christopher's reference on L3*r.* to p. 208 of Knox's *Elegant
Extracts*, which leads us to these lines in Parnell's 'Eclogue
on Health':

Here, wafted o'er by mild Etesian air,
Thou, country Goddess, beauteous Health! repair.

Wordsworth addresses the absent Coleridge:

For thou art wander'd now in search of *health*
And milder breezes, melancholy lot!
But Thou art with us, with us in the past,
The present, with us in the times to come:
There is no grief, no sorrow, no despair,
No languor, no dejection, no dismay,
No absence scarcely can there be for those
Who love as we do. Speed Thee well! divide

Thy pleasure with us, thy returning strength,
Receive it daily as a joy of ours;
Share with us thy fresh spirits, whether gift
Of gales *Etesian* or of loving thoughts.

(vi. 249–60)

One need not conclude from the Parnellian collocation of
health and Etesian gales that Wordsworth was directly
echoing that poet. Anyone who has read widely in the literature of a century in which men trained in the classics produced poems on such subjects as the art of preserving health
will be quick to point out that this association must have
been made many times. The significant point is not depen-
dent on these considerations. It is simply that Christopher's
notation helps us to see a truth about Wordsworth's poetry
and about the working of his imagination: that even when
he succeeded, as he boasted of doing in the Preface to the
Lyrical Ballads, in breaking up eighteenth-century clichés
of expression—and the passage in *The Prelude* shows the
accomplishment—the long reach of these clichés remained
in the yoking and collocation of ideas. Tradition emerges
even in the midst of newness and variety, a specific instance
is afforded of one of his avowed aims, and we are able to
contemplate the result in the light of the kind of original
materials with which he started.

Lyrics

Two of Wordsworth's lyrics have striking relationships with
Christopher's entries. We find on Np. 3, in obvious imitation
of 'L'Allegro', and also, as notations on Npp. 11 and 16 suggest, of *Midsummer Night's Dream*, several references to
folklore. One of these tells us that fairies 'frequently spin
for the maids'. One of William's songs gives us a direct
reflection of this localized version of a widespread folklore
motif:

63

Swiftly turn the murmuring wheel!
Night has brought the welcome hour,
When the weary fingers feel
Help, as if from fairy power;
Dewy night o'ershades the ground;
Turn the swift wheel round and round!
Now, beneath the starry sky,
Couch the widely scattered sheep;—
Ply the pleasant labour, ply!
For the spindle while they sleep,
Runs with speed more smooth and fine,
Gathering up a trustier line.

Short-lived liking may be bred
By a glance from fickle eyes;
But true love is like the thread
Which the goodly wool supplies,
When the flocks are all at rest,
Sleeping on the mountain's breast.

The Fenwick note tells us that this 'Song for the Spinning Wheel, Founded upon a Belief Prevalent among the Pastoral Vales of Westmoreland' was composed in 1806 and that Wordsworth had often heard the superstition on which it was founded from 'an old neighbour of Grasmere'. But in earlier editions he had dated it 1812, and Christopher's notations contain good reason for suspecting that, although he may have heard a Grasmere neighbour recount the superstition, he did not hear it from him for the first time, and that the statement about such a person in the Fenwick note merely provided that anchor in supposedly actual circumstance which Wordsworth's mind ever craved for themes which were essentially literary or at least unlocalized in origin.

Evidence in the notebook of a somewhat similar sort suggests that 'I Wandered Lonely as a Cloud' has likewise a formative history going much farther back than is usually supposed. Wordsworth says, again in a Fenwick note, that he wrote this poem in 1804, and de Selincourt says that it was clearly indebted to an entry in Dorothy's *Journals* under date of 15 April 1802, in which she tells us that on this date they discovered a great bed of daffodils on Ullswater and describes them in terms similar to those in the poem. Hence the conclusion which has been voiced by some readers that in part William only versified his sister's impressions and that she did the real poetic viewing of the flowers. But four points are worth noting. The first is that although Dorothy may have seen the Ullswater daffodils for the first time in 1802—but even this is hard to believe—we cannot imagine that a great body of flowers which grew by the side of a lake that Wordsworth began visiting as a schoolboy, which grew there during the whole period of his early life, and which was famous in the guidebooks of the time, was first seen by him so late as 1802. In the second place, on Np. 6 in collocation with a reference to the deer in Gowbarrow Park which turn up in *An Evening Walk,* we find Christopher making this entry:

> Daffodils. early in the spring. vast num
> bers of them by Ullswater side.

The third relevant consideration is found in a remark which Hazlitt made about *The Excursion* but which is equally applicable to much of Wordsworth's poetry: 'Every object is seen through the medium of innumerable recollections and clothed with the haze of imagination, like a glittering vapour.'[1] Finally, we happen to know a great deal about how another of Wordsworth's poems came into being, and what we know both confirms the justice of extending Hazlitt's remark and gives us a clue to what happened in 'I Wandered Lonely as a Cloud'. The poem is 'The Pass of Kirkstone'. The Coleorton copy tells us that it was composed 'chiefly in a walk from the top of Kirkstone to Patterdale', and on the back of it is written 'Mr. Wordsworth's verses, June 27,

---

[1] *Works,* ed. P. P. Howe (London and Toronto, 1930–4, 21 vols.), iv. 112.

1817'. Wordsworth himself says of this poem that it embodied 'thoughts and feelings of many walks in all weathers, by day and night, over this pass, alone and with beloved friends'. Here we have a poem composed during a specific walk and in a sense prompted by a specific expedition, but embodying recollections of many previous repetitions of the experience, both with and without others. I suggest that something analogous happened in 'I Wandered Lonely as a Cloud'. This poem was clearly not based only on the excursion of 1802 if for no other reason than that Dorothy was with him at that time, but if we think of it as composed then but embodying sensations of previous sights of the daffodils, perhaps, as the lines suggest, especially of his first view of them in boyhood, do we not have a conception of the poem thoroughly in accord with both known Wordsworthian practices and the content of the lines? If this may be accepted, I suggest that the similarities of phrasing in Dorothy's *Journal* are so far from representing sources of the poem as to be instead reflections of the materials of which it was made. A further conclusion is pointed at: the mere fact that an entry in the *Journals* precedes the supposed date of the composition of a poem does not establish in itself much of anything. Dorothy may only have been recording William's impressions for future poetic use.

The Guide to the Lakes

Though Wordsworth's *Guide to the Lakes* has usually been described as an unconventional work of its kind, it has many relationships with what one finds in the topographical writers and succeeded an earlier plan to 'describe a regular tour through this country, taking the different scenes in the most favourable order'.[1] It was, moreover, a journalistic money-making project, one of several such schemes which

[1] *Prose Wks.* ii. 101.

dotted his career from the beginning, and he admittedly incorporated in successive editions materials which he had by him for years. It seems probable that the plan was one which he long had in mind. Back of it and perhaps at one time coincident with it were *The Vale of Esthwaite* and *An Evening Walk*. A 'regular tour', furthermore, is close to being what the notebook and the 'Outline of a Poem' show Christopher to have been planning.

It is hardly surprising, therefore, to find William in the *Guide* citing Gilpin in support of his attack on painting houses white; commenting with appreciation on West's *Guide to the Lakes*; referring to Dr. John Brown and his Keswick *Letter*; giving us in full that writer's 'Night Piece' on Derwentwater, from which he had drawn in *An Evening Walk*; and quoting the conclusion of Gray's idyllic description of the Vale of Grasmere as that fastidious traveller saw it for the first time one Sunday morning. He draws materials, in short, from the same topographical writers from whom Christopher draws in the notebook.

The most striking relationship between the *Guide* and the notebook, however, emerges in connexion with what we may call the mountain-valley idyl. This was essentially a creation of the topographical writers, a kind of localization in the Lake district of Virgilian, Horatian, and Thomsonian themes, to say nothing of sentimental and primitivistic ones. The specific scene of this idealization of pastoral life and hospitality was most frequently Borrowdale, a circumstance for which Thomas Gray was responsible with his description in the *Journal* of the 'civil young farmer overseeing his reapers' at Grange-in-Borrowdale and the simple meal 'with butter that Siserah would have jumped at' with which he entertained the poet.[1] West followed closely in Gray's footsteps. In their mountain seclusion with their herds and flocks, fields waving with crops, and meadows 'enamelled

[1] p. 205. Here, as elsewhere, I follow the version of the *Journal* reprinted in West's *Guide,* the version referred to in the notebook.

with flowery grass', the inhabitants of Borrowdale, he declared, lived in a little delightful Eden, hospitable and friendly to those who visited their paradise, a striking example of 'the extensive influence of virtue in the minds of those that are least acquainted with society'.[1] Gilpin, too, was lyrical on Borrowdale and idealized life at Rosthwaite as Gray had at Grange.[2]

Borrowdale, however, was not the only setting of the idyl. Gray himself had found similar virtues elsewhere, as we learn from the famous passage, half picturesque landscape and half mountain-valley idyl, in which he describes his first view of the vale of Grasmere on a Sunday morning.[3] After this example, if any excuse were needed for the extension of the idyl to valleys like Patterdale, Langdale, and Buttermere, it was provided by West when he declared that 'all that Mr. Gray says of the young farmer at Grange is strictly applicable to the inhabitants of these mountainous regions in general'.[4]

With all their idealization, however, the Lake writers did not see the life of the dalesmen as free from dangers and accidents. Gilpin, with one eye on the Lake district and with the other fastened on Virgil and Thomson, pointed out that the shepherd's occupation exposed him to many difficulties and dangers in winter, that he was often obliged to tend his flock on the bleak side of a mountain, and that when snow came he sometimes was confronted with situations in which saving his flock meant risking his own life.

All the topographical writers trembled lest the simple virtue they described should be ruined by travellers and spoilers from the outside world; sometimes they lamented that this had already happened. Two attitudes, therefore, were possible toward the mountain-valley idyl—either that it existed, but was endangered, or that it had only recently ceased to exist.

[1] *Guide*, pp. 97–99. [2] *Observations*, i. 205.
[3] p. 211. [4] p. 93.

Such themes figure prominently in Christopher's plans. From the long entry which begins Np. 2 we learn that the exordium of the proposed poem 'In praise of the north' was to describe 'the simple, honest etc. manners of the country people', and to point out that hospitality 'etc. etc.' reigned in the Lake district. There are references to pastoral life and Borrowdale and Grange on Np. 15 and L3v., and further notations of a similar sort occur among the other entries. In Christopher's hands the idyl undergoes all sorts of amalgamations with other literary themes—the prelapsarian felicity of Adam and Eve, the king's speech in praise of the simple life in 3 *Henry VI*, country sports and festivities as described by Virgil and Thomson, the destructive autumn storm of those writers, and their tales of fair Lavinias adorning rural scenes.

Some of the relationships existing between these themes and Wordsworth's poems we have already examined and others are obvious—the Derwent-side bliss of the Female Vagrant in *Guilt and Sorrow*; the story of that 'artless daughter of the hills', the Maid of Buttermere, whose infant 'beside the mountain-chapel sleeps' in *The Prelude*; the 'sweet lass of the valley' who decorates the Helvellyn fair in the same poem; and that superb scene of bucolic festivity, with its dancing, wrestling, and racing, which the Poet and the Wanderer encounter in Langdale in *The Excursion*. There is, too, in the latter poem the portrait of Oswald, the mountain-valley youth, who with his strength and vigour and his excellence at country sports might almost be described as a sort of epitome of the entries on Np. 6. In the light of the mountain-valley idyl it appears, too, that such themes as the story of the man who perishes in the snow in *Descriptive Sketches* and the destructive autumn storm in the Coniston region which almost got into *The Prelude* were associated in Wordsworth's mind with this central conception.

It is, however, in the *Guide to the Lakes* that we can see

most clearly how directly the same topographical writers who made such an impression on Christopher moulded William's conception of the dalesman. The following passage, localized in no one dale but said to refer generally to the people who dwelt far up in the mountain valleys secluded from the world, is so completely in the manner of the Lake writers as to make it impossible to suppose it independently conceived:

Thus has been given a faithful description, the minuteness of which the reader will pardon, of the face of the country as it was, and had been through centuries, till within the last sixty years. Towards the head of these dales was found a perfect republic of Shepherds and Agriculturists, among whom the plow of each man was confined to the maintenance of his own family, or to the occasional accommodation of his neighbour. Two or three cows furnished each family with milk and cheese. The chapel was the only edifice that presided over these dwellings, the supreme head of this pure commonwealth; the members of which existed in the midst of a powerful empire like an ideal society or an organized community, whose constitution had been imposed and regulated by the mountains which protected it. Neither high-born nobleman, knight, or esquire was here; but many of these humble sons of the hills had a consciousness that the land which they walked over and tilled, had for more than five hundred years been possessed by men of their name and blood; and venerable was the transition when a curious traveller, descending from the heart of the mountains, had come to some ancient manorial residence in the more open parts of the Vales, which, through the rights attached to its proprietor, connected the almost visionary mountain republic he had been contemplating with the substantial frame of society as existing in the laws and constitution of a mighty empire.

(*Prose Wks.* ii. 62–63)

Certainly one hears Gilpin in this passage; one also hears Clarke on a felicity which had but recently passed away; and both Clarke and West on the chapel at Buttermere;

when we come to the traveller who journeys from the heart of the mountains to a manorial residence in the open parts of the vales, we are reminded irresistibly of the account in Gray's *Journal* of his progress from Borrowdale (3 October) to Sizergh Hall, the ancient seat of the Stricklands (9 October), and of Clarke's patently imitative descent from Buttermere to the lower reaches of the Vale of Lorton.[1]

Whenever it may have been composed, we can only believe that the passage embodies notions which were early in conception. They are essentially what Wordsworth started with in his view of the dalesmen. If we keep this fact in mind, we are in a position to observe certain other ramifications of the influence of the mountain-valley idyl in his works. For one thing, he was sometimes less inclined to emphasize the past quality of the valley felicity than to see it as still existing in his boyhood and youth and even in his maturity. We find this passage in *The Prelude*:

> For, born in a poor District, and which yet
> Retaineth more of ancient homeliness,
> Manners erect, and frank simplicity,
> Than any other nook of English Land,
> It was my fortune scarcely to have seen
> Through the whole tenor of my school-day time
> The face of one who, whether Boy or Man,
> Was vested with attention or respect
> Through claims of wealth and blood; nor was it least
> Of many debts which afterwards I owed
> To Cambridge, and an academic life
> That something there was holden up to view
> Of a Republic, where all stood thus far
> Upon equal ground, that they were brothers all
> In honour, as in one community,
> Scholars and Gentlemen, where, furthermore,
> Distinction lay open to all that came,
> And wealth and titles were in less esteem
> Than talents and successful industry.

[1] *Survey*, pp. 85–86.

71

Add unto this, subservience from the first
To God and Nature's single sovereignty,
Familiar presences of awful Power
And fellowship with venerable books
To sanction the proud working of the soul,
And maintain liberty.

(ix. 217–41)

There is more in these lines about Cambridge than about his
native vales, but the collocation of concepts is significant.
The references to the spare life of the district, the absence
of persons of rank, and 'mountain liberty' tell us clearly
enough that the valley idyl was in his mind and suggest
even that Cambridge, too, struck him as having something
of a republic about it because he was thinking of that other
republic, the 'almost visionary' one of the mountain vales.
Notions connected with it also underlie the important letter
which he addressed to Charles James Fox in January 1801,
with a copy of the second edition of the *Lyrical Ballads*. The
whole argument that a 'little tract of land serves as a kind of
permanent rallying point' for the domestic feelings and that
this way of life was threatened by changes operating at
the time is only a more philosophical and specialized statement of implications of the valley idyl. This conception,
moreover, underlies the two poems which Wordsworth
recommended to Fox's attention in what was essentially a
manifesto with a programme for political action—'Michael'
and 'The Brothers'. In commenting on the latter, he declared
that 'it was intended to be the concluding poem of a series
of pastorals, the scene of which was laid among the mountains of Cumberland and Westmoreland'.[1] It would appear
that at one time he intended to compose a series of poems in
which various aspects of the mountain-valley idyl would
have found illustration. If we could think of this plan as
having originated early, it would account for the curious
truncation in *An Evening Walk* of the theme of a 'Mountain

---

[1] *Poet. Wks.* ii. 47.

Farm' which is announced in the prose summary at the beginning, but is largely lacking in the poem itself.

We have now followed through the main relationships between William's works and Christopher's jottings. These connexions exist, as I have pointed out, independently of any explanations why they exist. I have been content to let the evidence largely speak for itself when seen through significant patterns of arrangement, juxtaposition, and progression, but I have attempted also to call attention to the processes of localization, amalgamation, fused transformation, and idealization that raw materials passed through in the creative process as we observe it in Wordsworth.

THE NOTEBOOK

NOTE

A PAGE-BY-PAGE type reproduction of the notebook follows this note. The text is also given line by line with interlinear additions printed as such and their approximate positions indicated. An exception is made in a few cases in which the jamming together of words or letters at the end of a line makes the observance of these principles impossible. The form used was dictated by the fact that any other involved the making of editorial decisions for which adequate data do not exist in the notebook. The spelling is that of the entries without editorial alteration. The punctuation is also that of the original, in which a mark in many cases indistinguishable from a period is used where a comma would seem appropriate. Because it is frequently not possible to determine which point the writer intended, this mark is regularly reproduced as a period, commas being used only where they clearly appear as such. The few notations in pencil made earlier than the main entries and therefore in some cases under them are so described in the Notes but are not separately distinguished in the transcription when they are clearly related in subject to the main body of the writing. The childish scribbling which disfigures a few of the pages has been omitted.

The following editorial devices have been used:

[?] an illegible word or words

[and?] a conjectural reading of a word or words.

Of the numerous editions of West's *Guide to the Lakes* the only one to which the page citations of the notebook exactly correspond is that of 1789. Gray's *Journal to the Lakes* is invariably cited with page numbers referring to the extensive Addenda in West's book, among which it appeared. Vicesimus Knox's *Elegant Extracts of Poetry* is referred to in the so-called Dublin 'third edition' of 1789. All page references to Thomson's *Seasons* appear to refer to the first volume of the *Works* (London, 1766, 4 vols.). Gilpin's Lake district *Observations* is referred to only indirectly and no citations of pages occur. This work appeared first in 1786 and had further editions in 1788 and 1792. That the third was not in mind is suggested by the fact that the issue of the *European Magazine* referred to on Np. 17 contains a review of this work. References to Clarke's *Survey of the Lakes* check with the second edition of 1789. On Np. 12 allusion is made to several of Joseph Farington's Lake district views. Though some of these were announced in a prospectus in the 1784 edition of West's *Guide*, and I have seen individual plates of this series with dates as early as the preceding year, they were published together for the first time in 1789. That they were out by April, we know from a dated preface in the edition of the *Guide* in that year.

W

His armour glittered in the
but fear sat on his forehead, as when
the sun shoots his beams upon
the side of skiddaw or helvellyn
but mists sette upon his head

Aug 22
1749

1 Storm at Legberthwaite.
sultry day. Autum. August. 7 o'clock
evening thunder lightening, rain
Helvellyn. vast stones.

2 Evening the sound of the torrent
the whirring & quaking of the grey
duck.

3 Oft have I walked till the
golden redness in the west fades
into the sober gray of the
evening, & even till twilight

4 Description of a sail upon
Windermere by day,
on derwent by night. Comb

In praise of the north Latin verse

There is a country in the north of England
consisting of Cumberland West. & Lancas.
of great beauty etc. Let no one travel to
see the boasted Alps or Switzerland Italy
or France before he shall have seen
these eminent beauties of his own
country. Besides here is much ad
vantage to be gained by observing
the simple, honest etc. manners of the
country people. hospitality reigns
here, etc. etc. This exordium. then descrip
tion of the Lakes, Mountains, Vallies,
Cascades. Rydal particular etc etc etc.
when read the Georgics
       of a maniac.
A Tale relative to Grasmere
   of   ning
Hawkshead. School. Praise of ler
Windermere. Echo. A Narration of
the drowning of some person
to inquire of Mrs. T. about this.
Rydal Lowdore. King of Patter
dale. Read Guide to the Lakes
Gays & Dr Browns Letters.
Call-garth. Superstition a distin
guishing trait in the character
of the North.
Description of robbing an eagle's nest
P. 206. G. Lakes

have been
Fairies are frequent here. 5   N
They are often seen sunning & counting their money. by the side of some
river or hill, in Grisdale near Patter
dale. Their dances. etc
They frequently spin for the maids etc
In Patterdale a man used always
to lay a piece of cheese (some rural
fare) & was always rewarded by
a piece of money in his shoe.
    Milton's l'allegro.
Description of Keswick Regatta

                                    6
Enquire about the tombstone on
one of the Windermere Islands
Callgarth. The sides of the walls are   7
covered with Ivy. & Wallflower.
Sycamores. The sculls lie in a win
dow of a large room cut out in
wood with various figures. one
of them is much broken.
The Bp. has planted near his new house
an immense quantity of
oaks. future forests shall wave.
                mentis gratissimus error
~~Conclusion.~~ This error of Fancy was
once frequent, but is now declining.
simplicity has yielded to civilization
which produces knowledge & conse-
quent incredulity.—

Gilpine

8 Description of the mists Beatties Mins.
Winter. Snow. sleet. rain. storm
Ice. etc. Storm description of.

9 No banditti haunt the mountains etc
But hospitality. 135 p. Guide to the L.
Borrowdale. Praise of an husband
man's & shepherds life. See 431 p. of
Eleg. Ex. Begin the day with thanks to God
for his blessings. & go to work with
the song of the lark. blithe themselves
singing etc
A description of the waterspout of
Septr. 1760 Lorton. Another happen
ned at St John's August 22d, 1749.
See Guide. L. p 140.

10
Description of the echoes produced
by guns etc in the mountaines
Ulswater Coniston

O

His crest nodded dreadful on
his head like an oak ~~on the Top~~
shook by the wind upon
the top of Teneriff—
As when the moon as she
when she [?]   [?]
raises her orb above the Horizon
rests upon the Branches of some
tall Oak, which grows upon
the summit of the Horizon

Description of the crags which fell at
Lowdore banks & blocked up the pass
age into Borrowdale. Gray's Journal
P. 203. G. L.

Lowdore waterfall   11

12
Description of an Evening: P. 206. G. Lakes
& Night

Guns & Music for Echo

13   activity
The vigour & strength of the youth
They climb the rock in search of
the lamb etc.
Their exercises, Leaping running
wrestling etc. dancing. &
Female beauty. etc. Hunting.
The fox. red deer. etc

14   early
Daffodils. in the spring, vast num
bers of them by Ullswater side.
G. Park. Deer. Run, then turn &
gaze at the passenger.

[The following entries in very faint
pencil are upside down at the bottom
of the page:]

To Derwent. Bowdar
Borrowdale. Lowdore [?]
Hunting the fox
Red deer & Fallow deer

The Thunder frequent strikes the
tops of the hills, & the sides.   15

In autumn misty evenening
the shepherd stalking over the
mountains, sees or thinks he sees
monsters through the mists. Or
rather, you if you should be
set there take the shepherd for a
giant.   16

Do these cataracts ever form rain
bows? Ask Leeson. Yes. Atkinson
Yes. Leeson.

17
In the spring morning, the lark
the thrush & blackbird sing.
The difft. character of Beauty which the
Lakes assume & the different ways by
which they interest at difft seasons
of the year. Spring. Summer. Autumn Winter

I dwell with delight upon the
scenes of my youth, I ~~hug~~ hug the
precious treasure, and cannot but
accuse treacherous Memory
for having left me so little. I stran
my fancy in amplifying, and
reducing to order the scattered
fragments. And If I shall have
found out some clearer happier
spot I dwell with pleasure upon
it, and only lament that it is
seen through as it were
such a dim vapour of years
which yet perhaps enhances
its value. As some wretch
driven out by a storm in a little
bark to sea, still the farther
he is carried, strains his eye
in feasting himself with a view
of the scarce seen distant land,
he suggests to his terrified
imagination, (while he just
scarce sees some beautiful promontory) the pleasures and the
joys which are now to him no
more, and the horrid storm
which is ready to swallow him
up. How different are the busy
the anxious the vicious, dangerous
hours of manhood, to the pleasing
innocent enjoyments of youth.

The Western shore of Windermere
is steep but of no great height,
rocky, & covered with frequent
hollies, ashes, & yews intermixed,
amongst which the blackbird
at morn & eve
& thrush sing & build their nests
& the wild pigeons, the hawk
& glead. Description of the rocky
and romantic scene [?] as we
approach the lake. Then West's 1st
station. It seemed to me that
a view a [piece?] on the far side
of Harrow, at the descent of
an hill on the road, was superior to West's secd. The view
upon the water up the lake
above B Grange is very fine.

18

Brother's Water. Narration
Clarke recommends Butter-lip
how Grasmere.
Slape crage Windermeres west
side
                  swarms
Summer the ceaseless hum of insects
Summe evening.

Clarke recommends
Butterlip how
Grasmere
Slape crage Winderm
west side.
    20.
No. 32. At the beginning of au-
        livid sky in the east. murky clouds
tumn. day sultry. and overshad
owed. a [?]unifying haziness.
a peal of thunder a sudden &
                the torrents descent etc.
most violent shower lays the
        drives the reaper from his work.
corn. surprizes the traveller. &
drives him to seek shelter. Thus
in life a sudden storm of
misfortune overwhelms us.

[Book?]
mighty was the warr[ior?]
dreadful was his countenance
yet it was tempered with the
placid serenity of deliberate
courage, as when a sun beam
gilds the top a rugged rock—
or when the sun skirts with gold
the top of some dark cloud—
They gaze upon each other
like two rocks which rise
from the sea in dreadful majesty
they stand unmoved while the
[waves?] dash at their feet, and
the Storm howls round their
heads.- - - - - - - - - - - - - -
Stood like a tower which at
dusky Evening the shepherd
views enlarged and magnified
by the darkness.- - - - - - - - -
Evening. Night. Elegant Extracts
Page. 387. 383. Mid. Nights Dream.

Could not I introduce an Hymn in Imi
tion of Milton's & Thompson's?

Stations. Windermere. Hill above the
ferry. Near Harrowslack.

South end of the ^{great} island down the
Lake. North end of d°. up the Lake.
Rawlinson's Nab. Hill above Bow
ness. A little behind Rayrigg.
(Near Rydal Hall.)
Opposite Bowness on the western
shore.   Pages   55 56   57
Clarke recommends Butterlip
     16 134   136
how Grasmere.

Slape crag Windermere. ^{on the} wes
tern shore
Grasmere Farington Opposite Helme
Crag. D° Windermere Gill Head   3
miles below Bowness. D° Directly
opposite Bowness on the Hill
D° Above Rarig, looking down.
D° Legberthwaite 6th milestone.
A few yards out of the road before you come
to the bridge, from Penrith, a picturesque
view of.

his consort is sad, the smile of
Joy forsakes her face, as when
_{of the earth}
the black shade interposes
betwixt the sun and Moon—

_{work labourer}
Two sculls. A Farmer at the
house about 20 years ago. affirms
that one night in Autumn he
_{another man}
& his family heard sweet music
in the air which seemed to move
about and at length to die away.
_{of the farmer}
The daughter fell sick the following
_{she thought she heard the music}
day & died immediately.   under her
                             bed
Various forms of spectres have at
difft times appeared.
     The sculls are said to have been those of
          [?   ] Collins
two poor people who used frequently to
go to Call-garth then the seat of the Phi
lipson's, for broken meat etc. who possess
ing a little field which the P. could
not, as the ardently wished procure,
or buy, they resolved however to get
it by whatever means. The poor woman
according to custom going for the meat
they put some silver spoons amongst it.
& after she was gone following her they found
them upon. accordingly she and her hus
band were executed. No. See next page.

One evening upon southerfell. there
were seen armed horse men galloping down the hill. etc. enquire of
this. they were seen twice. Clarke
mentions them. about 40 years intervened
between the times. once they appeared
only as horses, the other time (I believe
the latter) the year before the rebellion
as a regt. of soldiers on horseback.
they thought the they heard breathing, & run
ing of the horses

They were involved in a law suit
by which they were entirely impoveris
hed.

At their death they left the 109 psalm
to the Philipsons, who accordingly
were reduced to beggary, & to a vaga
bond life, from affluence & pros
perity. Discite justitiam.

Even handed justice
Returns the ingredients of our poison'd chalice
To our own lips.

21. Mines. Coniston C. Newland Lead
   & C. Borrowdale. Wad:
22 Pastoral Life Borrowdale, Lang
   dale. Buttermere etc.
   Keswick. Brackenthwaite etc
23. Flocks & Herds. Hospitality.
24: Scale force 56 yards. Trees. Birch etc

25. Are you an admirer of extensive views ascend Skiddaw
or Grasmire. And see moun
tains, vales, the sea etc below you.
Consider the busy, various scene
beneath you. But these are
often infested with storms etc
which perhaps may drive
you ignominiously into the
vallies. Sweeter scenes, & calm
serenity etc await those in the vale.
As in life the ambitious etc etc.
Whilst the contented enjoy quiet etc

A Whirlwind in 1790. carried some
sheep (2 I believe) off Coniston Fell.
The Hay. is often carried up
into the air. in summer.
26.
Then oft (in Winter) the peasauts
at night, while the storm roars around,
in a circle converse about witches etc.
Introduction concerning superstition.
27.
Grasmere morning. Windermere
               x
Noon. Derwent. Evening & Night.
Ulswater. Storm.
28X Evening. Night. Elegant Ext. Page
  383. 387. Mid Sum. Nights dream
29
  The beams of the moon in the water
seen at a distance. the moon her
self in the water.
30.
  Oft at the beginning of autumn
are these partial storms.
in the vales whilst the moun
tain top is clear. and they surprize
the traveller when he least expects
them. See the former leaf. No. 32

[Starting at the bottom of the page and
upside down are the following entries in
faint pencil under the foregoing ones in
ink:]
         [?]thwaite
        Lowdore

[Page 16 cont.]

9 [?   ]
[?] [?   ]
6 [Keswick?]
[?] [?   ]
8 [Matterdale?]
[4?] [Patterdale?]
10

Evening. The reflection of the mountains
etc in the lake. See Gilpin. 31. Eu. Mag. Jan. 88.

- -

After the descriptions of Morning
32. Noon etc. shew the effects which
the difft. seasons produce. conclude
winter. its storms, frost, scaiting.
            Addison's Latine poem.
on Esthwaite. Fired with the
thought etc Praise of Learing etc
& Hawkshead. etc etc. End
Fishing. hunting. cooing dove.
Rose. Honeysuckles salute the nostrils
as slowly I wander by. Summer— 33.
In summer reclined under thy
trees or seeking thy lake to cool
my fervid limbs.   34
Oft Hd. have I heard the last evening song
of the thrush in thy Groves. matin.
Oft have I watched with impatience
the buds & the blossoms of spring,
which when they had appeared, it delighted
me to lead my wildly devious way.
Along thy banks oh Winder. Conis. Esth.
Gras. Rydal. Cas. etc. 34.
I have often watched the sun setting, & the last beam
upon the eastern hills, & the slow shades of night
invest the pole. The Moon.
The expiring song. cuckow etc. the last
red fade in the west & sober grey
succeed. the watch dog. the owl. or the
voice sounding accross the lake.

Spring. Snow-drops. Daisies. Primroses
Daffodils. Cuckow. 35.
Description of a man perishing in
the snow. 36.

creeping on his knees
one almost dead reaching to his home [speechless?]
till warmth restore his limbs
have 37.
I felt along thy banks, what time

in
at Eve the spring the birds etc When
[?]
the horizon was contracting, & the soft
shour yet hanging dubious, which
conferred a kindly gloom, O Esthwaite
sensations, such as would that I
might often feel. I have joined
my voice to that of the birds flocks etc
to thank my Maker.
say shall not Man pour out the
song of gratitude when he knows
the source from whence all these
blessings arise to their author since

glad
all the creation welcomes the approach
of spring. I counted in the long Room
one day 437 eggs
Spring. Oft have I watched the wood pigeon
The thrush's etc nests. but never plundered
them. Never my little schoolfellows
let the widowed dove etc. pour out her
moan. & curse you ravaging hands.
Think to yourselves with what grief *your* Mother
would be afflicted. sh. the cruel spoiler death
snatch *you* from her

S

before Winter is expired
He loved the fair Elfrida, but
their love was mutual
her Sire denied the completion
of their happiness, as when
[?] reclines upon the
The Spring ~~throws her~~ arms
lap of the youthfu
round the Youthful Year, the
hoory Winter rears his icy arm
and dashes her from his embrace.
Soft South wind. warm rain. Evening.
sun breaks out. verdure. Birds. all human
Nature rejoices.
Spring. 38. While oft the west
wind roars & brings hail etc
and blackens all the vale
while short gleams of sunshine
burst forth & serve to divide
the showers. Ev'n then 'tis
sweet when perhaps at Eve the
storm has ceased, the wind
yet blowing amid the trees
& the sun shining while
the clouds scoul down the sky
to meditate etc.
Turrita nubes. shaped like towrs

Queries. Are the tops of the mountains
ever serene & free from storms, while
the storm is raging on their
sides? Yes Atkinson
Is there any Tale, or has there
ever any thing particular happened here?
What time do the greatest floods happen?
Description of them.

blasts
Are there ever any whirlwinds here?

waterfalls
Are there any echoes? Any cascades here?
Do not the mists appear strange?
At what time of the year?
Did you ever see round rainbows?
Are there ever any persons drowned here
Or lost in the snow? shepherds?

Dal[t?]on. D[oe?]ton. Walney horn
for bell. Walney souls soles
& [?]. Walney criterion of
bad halfpence. [Dalton dollor?]
[a?] guinea restoring man to
youth. Prejudice agst. [shooting?]
flying

Flattering companions are Dangerous

[*Recto*]

Autumn. Storm. No. 8. 15.
16. 20. 30. Thompson's
Seasons p. 126. 148. 88.
Gilpin
Georgics.
Mists. Beattics Min. Seasons. 139.

(Difft characteristics & [?]
description of morning
noon, evening
Spring summer, Au-
tumn mists, elaborate,
storm. Winter)
Storm Lucretius P. 9.
Spring. Flor. Poet. 14.

Windermere. then, charac
teristics to Winter. Ice
the striving youth
such as I oft have felt on
thee oh Esthwaite.
Fired at the name etc
Nor shalt thou pass unsung.
particularly elaborate.

The conduct of the human
understanding

[*Verso*]

Lacuum in Cumbriâ, Westmoriâ et comitatu.

Lancastriensi sitorum, atque agri quoque in quo positi sunt descriptio.

<small>qua</small> <small>siti sunt</small>

Thompson's Seasons.   Club.
Denham. C. Hill

Elegant Ex. Page. 4. İ0, Ӟ4. 134 15İ. 173. 208. 221. 225. 283. 356 etc. 489. 383. 387.
Ode pop. superstit. Lucretius. etc. Georgics

[Recto]

13.   12
St Mathew 5, 6, 7. 25, 26, 7. 8—St Mark 1, 13—St Luke 2, 9, 15,
                    the whole of the gospel
          Construe these into Latin, when [?   ] [in English?]
16, 23, 24—St John. 1, 11, 14, 5, 6, 17, 19, 20—Acts 26, 27—
Romans 2, 8, 12.—1 Cor. 2, 9, 13, 15—2 Cor. 4, 6, 11—Ephes
4, 5, 6. Philipp. 1, 2, 3—Colloss 1, 3. 1 Thess. 2, 5. 1 Tim 1, 6.—
2 Tim. 2, 3. Heb. 1, 4, 6, 11, 12. 1 St Peter all. 2 St Peter all

[*Verso*]

                    a vulture preying upon
his stomach, for such is continual apprehension.
The gloomy mind fabricates its own tortures, and
by a studious endeavour to avoid, falls into tenfold
unhappiness.

   He seems too sensible of the futility of Fortunes
gifts, but though he is so, yet he is wrongly
sensible, for he so much the more vainly attempts
to render them perfect and lasting.

[Between the lines of the foregoing entry and upside
down are the following ones:]

[Dall ?]

Non Famae splendor, seu Laudis gloria quemquam
   Neve Decus vanum, pallida morte tenet

[*Recto*]

~~9. 22. 3.~~   7. 26. 16:   5.

Manners. (Superstition. Fairies. ~~under~~

Thompsons. Seasons, P. 186.

a digression, at Callgarth [1.?] <u>Ode on pop. super</u>)

(Deserted Village. [Health?] Eleg. Ex. [208?]

Diversions. Sports. Exercises. Fox hunting.

Red Deer. Leaping. Wrestling. Running.

Pastoral life. T. Seasons, 158, 175, 157, 158.)

27. 32.

(Different characteristics of beauty in

Thompson's Hymn.

the difft seasons of the year. ~~Storm.~~

17. 35. 38.   19   [~~P.?~~] ~~15. 16. Storm.~~

Spring   Summer. ~~Autumn~~ ∧ . Winter.

~~29. 30.~~36

Ice.)

~~2.~~12. 28–9.   10   11.   24

31.   Echo   Waterfall.

Evening

31

~~3.~~ 33–4. 37. ~~2~~   14   18.   4.   6.

Hawkshead.   Ulswater.   Windermere.

4.

~~Derwent.~~ (Skiddaw. Grongar hill).

                Apostrophe to the river Derwent.

Embellish it with classical allusions etc

101

[Verso]

Morning. Mist. (not the elaborate description)
birds singing. all joy & gladness. what
a contrast to the scene we saw last night
We will proceed under Barrow etc to Lowdore
_{Grange}   _{Bowdar.}   _{Manners}
then to Borrowdale. Eagle Nest. Pastoral
     _{Sports etc.}
life, etc etc. This seen, I would carry
you to Skidaw etc. To Bassenthwaite. a
short description. To Crommack. Scaleforce etc a short description. We would
wander among the hills, round the lake
         _{sailing upon it}
etc etc cross the meadows. along Derwent
side. Apostrophe to that river. but
alas! in life nothing is to be enjoyed long
we must leave these delicious scenes. Fare-
     _{every   good   wish.}
wel to Keswick.   Set out for Thirlmere etc.

[Under the foregoing entries in ink and at right angles to
them is the following equation in faint pencil:]

Given $\underline{x}$ plus $\underline{x}$ plus $\underline{x}$ equals d. To find x.
      a   b   c

x plus $\underline{ax}$ plus $\underline{ax}$ equals ad
       b   c

bx plus ax plus $\underline{axb}$ equals abd
                 c

bcx plus axc plus axb equals abcd

bc plus ac plus ab times x equals abcd

Therefore x equals $\underline{abcd}$

                    bc plus ac plus ab

102

[On the upper right side, at right angles to the entries in ink and upside down with respect to the equation, is the following date, apparently that of an old letter from which this sheet was salvaged:]

[dec?] 1771

APPENDIX

Christopher Wordsworth's 'Outline of a Poem'

Outline of a Poem descriptive of the lakes etc. Febry 1792
Ille terrarum mihi praeter omnes Angulus ridet. Horat.

I sing lakes, woods & mountains, & the charms of a
delightful country. O Muse assist my weak endeavours lest
my unfledged wing be unequal to the attempt. I confess
myself unequal to the attempt, & had not you my friend
impelled me to it I should have relinquished it, but the voice
of friendship persuades me to it, *(& I haste to conduct you,
& be your guide to these lakes the glory of rugged Westmorland, of Cumberland distinguished for the vigour and
courage of its men, & Lancashire for the beauty and charms
of its women.) Nor am I ignorant (Nec me animi fallit) how
uncouth many words will sound in Latin verse, & particularly with me an unskillful votary of the muses. But if you
must you may laugh. You cannot expect from me the description of scenes which would require the pen of Maro,
but what I can I will. *I haste then etc—above.

When Spring has advanced in the green plains, when the
woods are clothed in their richest foliage, etc. etc even then
leave the environs of the smoaky, noisy town; shut for a while

104

your books, & come & read with me the book of nature. As her rich stores, she opens them to your inquisitive eye, look & admire.

We will begin from Penrith, here mounting our horses (for I hate the chariot which obstructs our view, at early morn we will sally out towards Ulswater, passing by Dalemain the beautiful seat of Mr Hasell & with the Emont, which issues from the lake, at a small distance from the road we proceed through thorn hedges & enclosures to the lake. Here, if you please we will mount Dunmallet, a conical hill, clothed with wood & view the lake extending for some miles into a deep recess closed by the hills of Martindale to the south west, in a beautiful prospect, on the east side a beautiful border of woods & enclosures to the side of the lake fenced behind with a parapet of mountains, on the west side are some smooth topped hills (after which) edging down to the lake, after which succeeds Wate[r]millock the estate of Mr or Capt Robinson, the uncle of H. whom you well remember. This Hill (Du[n]mallet) on which we stand is said to have been a Roman station, of which there were a chain to repell the fierce attacks of the wild *Picts.* Descending from hence I will conduct you by Watermillock on the west side of the lake; from whence within half a mile the second reach of the lake opens, in magnificent grandeur. the reach lies immediately in front of a good breadth & to a great extent, on the left, the east side, are mountains, steep *Here the trumpet has sounded, & the fierce Roman conqueror of the world trod. Echo terrified has screamed to the tuba or the lituus. may no such sounds ever again infest these vales, but may they enjoy quiet content & peace. [*] lofty & rugged, descending in some parts almost perpendicularly into the lake, without any border of cultivation; on the west, pursuing the road, after descending a little hill we enter Gowbarrow park, park-like ground on which are herds of cattle feeding, & the deer oft running away & then

turning to gaze upon the passing traveller. about the midway in this reach is Lyulp's tower in a grand situation built
by the duke of *Norfolk.* Here for a while we will bid adieu
to the lake & turning near the tower into the wo[o]ds we
                through a narrow glen
will be conducted, the river roaring at our feet, to Airey
                      thundering noise
cascade, which falls with a roaring sound into a deep hollow
bason, almost overshadowed with trees. Description of a
rainbow formed in the specus adverso sole. Then leaving
Gowbarrow park, we pass through some fields, cross a
bridge near Glencoine & enter Westmorland. Presently
some noble woods of oak Ash Birch etc will receive us &
under their shelter, delighted with the singing of birds, we
will proceed, one *Echo produced by the report of a gun
repeated nine or ten times, etc. Lucretius, P. 115. [*]
‡ Visit the cascade upon our return.
while looking down upon the deep black lake beneath us,
again, looking up with terror upon the rocks which hanging
over our heads threaten to crush us, or often from some little
eminence feasting our eyes with a noble view of the reach
we have passed or looking forward to the last reach which
has now received us. the woods passed we enter patterdale,
a sweet sequestered spot. O my friend shouldest thou ever
in disgust with the world, its crimes, its vices, its follies,
should thy fine breast feel keenly the slighted regard of
despairing merit, scorned by the haughtiness of the proud,
treated with ingratitude by a friend, or slighted by your
mistress, retire hither. see the hand of God in all his works,
            torrent
the cascade, the storm, the grove, spring, summer, Autumn,
winter 'talk of him in solitary glooms,' mount that hill, follow
this rivulet etc. etc. labour this. Every day see new beauties
etc etc. But far be it from me to recommend solitude. I think
most pleasure may be reaped in social life, among sisters,
brothers, children & friends, & from a quiet conscience.
/The frequency indeed, the multiplicity & sometimes per-

haps the enormity which occurs in the great world may perhaps be unseen here, but alas the reign of vice is far spread, & even here she has some sway/. Here reigns the

king of patterdale, whose dominions, in comparison with the pride of Windsor or Versailles hide their diminished heads, but the palace or the dwelling cannot ennoble the abject mind the present king is a votary at the shrine of Plutus. I indeed, if I wished to reign, it should be in Patterdale; where there is no ambition, no perfidy, no dethronement, no rebellion, no murders, poisonings, imprizonments. I would fish upon Ulswater, or mount Placefell etc & look down upon my kingdom, my cattle, my woods, etc. shoot & hunt.

Here are many grains, each of which, would you follow them would afford something entertaining or striking, which terminate in mountains browzed upon by numbers of sheep the wealth of this country. next page.

~~Storm~~. We will leave the palace on our right hand, pass the modest chapel, above which the vale divides into several after grains etc. one of which leads over Kirkstone to Ambleside. Here if you please we will turn our horses again & enter the inn. Here we should stay some time, nay even years to form an adequate idea of the beauties of the country. Not as most do, come here to eat a dinner & then return. Though unwilling we must however return, & trace back again our course. by the way we will visit Airey force. # Return to Penrith.

Thence to Keswick. Mosedale beck inundation* &*

Southerfell sights. rebellion Pass Threlkeld. Thomp. Seasons, 154 Druidical monument in a field on the left hand of the road. Mosedale is a little Beck that rizes in Hellvellyn, joins Grisdale beck, & joins St John's beck. We would cross it in going between Threlkeld & Patterdale. It was worst in Legberthwaite. It descended down Helvellyn on both sides. disrupit rupes.

Saddleback
*Southerfell joins Helvellyn, is a smooth sided mountain of considerable height.

The Greeta when they join is considerably larger than the Derwent. it keeps its course, & it is the Derwent which makes an angle & runs into it.

[&c. morning mist?]
Keswick. Vale. Opens to us soon after this is passed
Hail to thee queen of vales etc.   a general view of the valley.
Skiddaw rises on the right. The descent is by a gentle declivity at a small distance from the town where we meet

Greeta
the river [----?---]. First, we will refresh ourselves in the inn. Walk out in the evening to the side of the lake. Come away; let us leave the bottle & the table, we are called to richer and manlier luxuries. Even now the Sun is declining. Sol inclinas. let us away to the banquet of the senses. let us betake ourselves to the shore of the lake. to Crow park.

I think
(even* now the sun gilds the rugged sides of Wallow-crag & now he is sunk beyond the western hills.) Here islands verdant or clothed with wood, mountains up whose steep

scattered cottages,
sides the richest wood is creeping, the smooth surface of the
the boat with its [?]
lake reflecting the opposite shore, rich fields & all illumined

golden
by the rich rays of the setting sun present to the eye a most luxurious picture, view at a distance of the white foam of Lowdore, the lofty Skiddaw your background, & the picture bounded by the Castle crag & the vast mountains of Borrow-dale.

when the fiery red is fading in the west, & yellow to
*Even now while the shades of evening are advancing &
the brown [?]
wrapping about to wrap all in a leaden obscurity, we will sit us down or wander slowly on the shore. See Hesper glitters

stars
in the west. the lights of heaven are now lighting up; See the moon full-orb'd appears above yon hill, & with soft light

shadowy sets off the face of things, see in long stream of light she shoot[s] along the lake; stopping frequent, with held breath, listen [to] the sullen sound of the fishermans oar striking the water, hear the watch-dog, Lowdore born in varied tones upon the breeze; this my friend is a scene of solemnity, a scene of repose that beggars all description. But hist! do you not hear yon sounds of music, that kiss our ravished ears, is it enchantment? hear you that dying fall & stealing over the lake those hundred echoes speaking from the hills? Sweeter far than the harp of Orpheus or of Linus or Musaeus, it is the horns which I ordered without your knowledge to play in it gives even a presentiment of heavenly joys the evening. Would you change this scene for all that cities, ball-rooms, palaces can bestow [?] Do not you feel your heart swell with rapture & devotion, & take part with free from all mortal cares, our breast sympathize in the calm the quiet of the scene [?] Contemplation here might woo his God.

In the morning, by sun rize, we will mount our horses & leave the enfeebling down. We will set out, on the east side along of the lake for Borrowdale. See now as we go along how the mists are clearing-off before the Sun. all is joy & gladness. What a contrast to the scene we saw last night! The choir of the linnet, finch, black birds, the opposite shore reflected in the calm bosom of the bird, Thrush lake, the whole country in all its beauty, the dew drops yet hanging on the trees, the richest perfumes from the Cynor-rodon (wild rose) & honey suckle etc etc. We will proceed salute the nostrils to Lowdore. Description of this boasted fall. After Rain, the under Barrow [?] sun breaking out. See Eleg. Ext. P. 225. Soon after this we there enter Borrowdale under rocks threatening to crush, in the interstices of which are several difft. sorts of trees. See on the other side of the river is the Grange. Bowdar stone on the right hand of the road. A beautiful vale environed with most tremendous mountains many covered with trees, beautiful meadows through which the Derwent clear as glass wheels vorticibus crebris his rapid course. In these rocks the eagle builds his nest. From hence he ravages the fields, flying off to his young with hares, lambs & partridges.

built in vast crags
Taking of the eagles eyrie. The whole dale is in arms, to terrify the eagle with shouts etc or fire at him if he should attempt to attack the plunderer, who is commonly some young shepherd let down by ropes, the old eagle indignant screams and wheels around his flight often threatening

the chapel
death to the plunderer of his young. Above [?] the vale divides & is now no longer passable, it becomes more wild than ever, scarcely a patch of cultivation, but nameless mountains, or known only to the shepherds, & glens where the sun scarcely ever shines, (afford the finest pasture for sheep) where no sound is heard but the barking of the eagle, the dashing of the torrent, or the bleating of sheep. For to tend these, to follow them when gone astray, attended by their faithful dog, to take care of the lambs etc and all the pastorial care, is all the care they know; they climb the mountain, & gather health from the breeze in the evening they return home welcome to their smiling family; little know they of the madding world, its wars its dissensions, & its tumults; they have not learned to wander in the maze of science, even the book of nature they view with careless eyes: contentment is all they know, an easy heart is their riches. sometimes they are compelled to endure great hardships in severe winter in gathering in their sheep from the storm, sometimes they are lost in the snow, & sometimes they can scarce reach home speechless & crawling upon their knees, their blood being frozen by the cold. But of this they are soon forgetful. After a sheep shear-

ing they give loose to joy, in dancing with a blooming partner.

In wrestling, cudgelling, or leaping, while the virgins sidelong look animates their vigour, & cheers their sinking soul.

Thus they pass their life, content, healthy, & vigorous, but yet though few their wants their pleasures are but few etc. Their character, give them exactly the same as Goldsmith gives the Swiss in his Traveller. Flor. Poet. 54.

These seen ni piget I would carry you through various excursions, first down to Bassenthwaite along the side indented with bays & promontories, varied with woods & fields etc etc.

Then through Newlands to Buttermere, Crommack, & Loweswater, vast mountains upon a very grand scale, rich vallies and fields, composing many delightful views, here are herds & waving harvests along the side of the Cocker etc. Here are you fond of fishing the trout will afford excellent sport. Here also we will visit O Scaleforce, though [*sic*] the lord of waterfalls, whose roaring even silences that of the boasted Lowdore himself. Shaded by a few birch etc.

These seen I would carry you to Skiddaw

Clarke, Page 55. I shall describe this remarkable phenomenon nearly in the words of Mr. Lancaster of Blakehills from whom I had the account; On 23d of June 1744, his father's servt. Dan. Stricket about 1/2 past 7 in the evening as he was walking a little above the house saw a troop of men riding on Southerfell side (a place so steep that an horse can hardly travel on it at all) in pretty close rank & at a brisk walk. S. did not for some time dare to go to point out what he saw to any one as the year before he had made himself ridiculous by a similar visionary story, which was in substance thus. Sitting at the door one evening, after supper with his then master John Wren of Wilton hill they saw a man with a dog pursuing at an amazing pace some horses along S. fell. Going the next day to see they did not find the least vestige. This story after having concealed for some time they at length told, & were heartily laughed at. Stricket therefore observed these aerial troops some time before he ventured to mention what he saw. At length however fully satisfied he went & told it to his master who saw it likewise, whereupon they called the rest of the family who all saw this strange phenomenon.--Mosedale-Beck inundation

P. 57. Mosedale Beck inundation. August 22d, 1749. It descends on the left side going to Keswick a little beyond the 11th milestone between Wolf-crag & Dodd, two mountains. All the evening of that [day] tumultuous noises were heard in the air, sometimes a puff of wind blowing with violence & in a moment all calm again. The inundation awaked the inhabitants, about 1 A.M. the rain began & by

in particular Legber. mill

4 all was desolation, houses washed away, people forced to climb to the roof to save themselves, & even then in danger of being carried way with their houses, trees torn up by the roots etc. etc. rocks split. Thunder and Lightning began about nine o'clock. Sulpherous smell in the air. The flashes were uncommonly large so that the air was in a contin. glow.

Skiddaw. Are you fond of mountain prospects we will ascend the celebrated Skiddaw; as we wind round his sides, see the prospect swell around, we look down with contempt on the scenes we have just been admiring the lake is diminished to a pool, the rivers are scarcely discernible

how close the ridges lie

winding in meanders through the vale; we see new lakes,

The sea.

new vales, & new mountains like a tumultuous ocean; here now as we stand upon this summit let us look down upon the world, could we as we are exalted above the vales, so be raised above everything mean & sordid, could we look down with contempt upon the petty cares of that little, busy toiling insect man, twere well, but see! as now we are philosophizing here, the mist arises, the wind howls over the desert, darkness settles around us, come away! we are

driven down again in ignominy to the vales below to associate with our fellow creatures: vain is the pride of conceited
philosophy; to know ourselves that we are but men, like
others, is true knowledge, vain is the pride of empty ambition. See how she tempts one wretch with the false glitter of
unreal honours, see how he pants he struggles to grasp them;
see how she tempts him to where she holds them out upon
yon precipice, see how he, heedless of his feet, attempts to
seize them, his foot slips, he tumbles to the bottom to bitter
scorn a sacrifice & grinning infamy. For me, indeed, I prefer
the calm, quiet more beautiful scenes of the vales, than these
of climbing the mountains which seldom I think repay the
trouble.

climb

All these seen we wander among the vallies, mount every
hill for a new prospect, walk round, & along the banks of
the lake, sail upon, & anchor in every bay & upon every
island, roam through the woods, among the meadows, &

is   on

along the side of the Derwent. thou not the least noble of

though he rolls his throug Tempe

rivers, thou who enviest not the Peneus, [Arno?] nor the Po.
thou along whose side my careless childhood oft has strayed,
when I had yet no fear of ills, no care beyond today. But
alas! it is not given us in this life to enjoy aught long. We
must leave, my Friend these delicious scenes. Now as we

turning round

ascend this hill, ere yet we turn out of sight, let us feast our
eyes again with the prospect, let us bid adieu! & wish to
Keswick every good wish. Farewell sweet vale, Skiddaw,
Lowdore, Borrowdale & Derwent farewell. ~~But~~ We must
leave with feelings not unlike what we experience at passing from a beloved friend.

With sad hearts let us turn our eyes to the scene before
us we are now in Legberthwaite a narrow pleasant valley,
see huge Hellvellyn's brawny sides to the left etc. at the
milestone turn & have a view of the vale behind a noble

view bounded by the mountain saddleback. Then we proceed, soon come in sight of ~~the lake~~ Thirlmere, a long lake
divided in two & the sides joined by a rude bridge
environed on all sides with rude mountains, here is scarce
cultivation
a trace of vegetation to be seen, but all is rugged, silent, gloomy. After a storm the torrents rushing down the sides of the mountains, foaming white, the face of many rocks illumined by a partial gleam of sunshine, & the dark bosom of the lake present a most romantic picture, & the bird of Jove screaming over our heads.

This passed we cross Dunmail-raise remarkable for a battle fought From hence we look down at a distance upon the sweet vale of Grasmere. A most delightful contrast to the scene which we have just left. Here all is sweetness, quiet & serenity. Surely not more beauteous was the vale of
where   gathering
Enna with proserpine wandered with her companions, &
flowers
touched the iron heart of Pluto etc. See Metam. B. 5, V. 384, & Flor. Poet. 71. A neat island rises in the lake, neat cottages are scattered along the margin, & a neat church is seated at a little distance from it.

This hill descended, will bring us to Rydalmere a small lake, this is in the gloomy stile. Here is an antique mansion the seat of the noble family of the Flemings. A fine forest of wood. The cascades.

a
Hence to Ambleside ~~two~~ mile.
Windermere.

Thus, my Friend, we have arrived nearly at the end of our journey, not a little pleased, I hope, with the beauties we have seen. But these are not all. There are many occasional beauties which seldom occur, many which result from the seasons, many which will escape you at the first, & new ones which will appear at every succeeding view, so that I am persuaded one might spend here without satiety a whole life, & even with daily increasing delight. Morning. Noon & Evening.

At the approach of spring when the gentle zephyr relaxes the soil, how delightful is it to wander by the side of some lake, the thick rack standing dubious upon the hills, & casting a pleasing gloom upon the scene, the air warm, & the surface of the lake undisturbed by a single breath of winds, to hear the woods resound with the voices of a thousand ^the^ songsters; to mark the springing ~~blade~~, ^cuckow^ ^herb^ the snowdrop primrose, daisy & daffodil, & at the expiring song to retire home in sweet meditation, our heart rejoicing as all nature rejoices, & swelled with gratitude to our great & bountiful creator. Flor. Poet. 14.

In summer how delightful to catch the light breeze in the bosom of the sail, to cool our tepid limbs in the translucent lake, or under the broad umbrage of some sycamore or oak to listen to the ceaseless hums ^swarms^ of innumerable insects. the beetle. hawthorne hedge.

In autumn. In the morning mount the top of some hill & view the whole country around covered with a white mist, sometimes level, & extended like a plat of Ice or snow with the tops of the hills peeping above it, sometimes rolling in billows below, unveiling one part of the valley while another is yet in obscurity, while the crowing cock, the barking cur, the lowing kine, & the clock ^bell^ from the distant church are heard proceeding from we know not whither.

In autumn too, day sultry, & overcast, ^livid sky in the east^ ^gloomy & dark^ in the groves aridus fragor a peal of thunder, the lightning strikes Hellvelyns side, & the echoes return the sound, the collision of clouds, the elemental war; the lightning sometimes lays prostrate the sheep, or blasts the oak or ash, the whole atmosphere descends in rain, deluges the fields, lays prostrate the corn,

the river rushes down the dell spreading desolation, hark
how Scaleforce and Lowdore roars. What sublimity! The
Storm Lucretius page 9th. Virgil Geor. 1.
suppliant heart with adoration reveres the mighty parent of
storms etc. Are your [*sic*] fond of meditation here is a fund
for it, learn from hence that the hand which gives blessings
can also punish the guilty.
Vide Addend.
hail
In Winter. Snow sleet & rain roaring ~~with~~ [?] strepitu
present nature in her awful view, even here, in desolation,
there is food to delight the eye, the ear & the senses.

But when these storms have yielded to frost, & when he
binds in icy chain the lake, let us hasten to the side & take
the diversion of skaiting. Addison's poem, where the youth
in fond emulation strive in ardent race animos in ponunt.
such as I have often felt on thee oh Esthwaite.

name
Fired with the ~~sound~~
Thee also I will sing, thou not the least in the beauties of
nature, for thou also hast a lake, woods & pleasant fields
but thou art chiefly eminent for an ancient & respectable
seminary of learning. Mark where that mansion rears its
of his [centum.?]
modest front, there science for upwards 200 years has fixt
her seat, & there the youth of ages have been educated
some
~~themselves~~ studious of honest praise have emulously
struggled to distinguish themselves in the liberal sciences,
some have shone among their fellows & gained the palm
vid. addend.
gramineâ palestrâ. for wrestling, running, leaping etc &
some observing the wise men have made themselves at once
learned, & strong; about to shine in the senate or the field
in private or public life, in the bustle of the world, or the
leisure of a retired life; and have shewn themselves sons
worthy of Britain. Here, I also, from my earliest years have
been educated [?] tenues haustus at the fount of learning,

116

enamoured of science. Here oft with impatience I have watched the approach of spring, its buds & blossoms which when they had appeared it de[lighted] me to wander devious I scarce knew whither.

Then oft when the sky was contracting, & the soft shower yet hanging dubious, which conferred a kindly gloom, when the birds were singing in thousands through the grove, &
the cuckow, the moaning dove
the innocent lambs were frisking in playful mirth around, & when all nature in joy & gladness hailed the return of spring, then have I felt the purest sentiments of joy & gratitude to God, my heart swelled, I joined my own voice to that of the songsters, & poured out my heart in secret, oh solitude thou bringest the heart to itself & teachest it wisdom etc.

Thus have I wandered along the lake, & (coasting with tardy steps the side of the still lake), oft have outwatched the last sun beam on the eastern hills, & the [?] redness in the west in the sweet converse of friends, or alone & coasting with tardy steps, nor even retired before the night had fuscis alis overshadowed the earth after the song had expired in the grove & leaden darkness had covered the whole, standing by the shore, listening to the distant torrent
the quaking and whirring of the duck
born upon the air, the owl, the watchdog, or the voices sounding from the farther shore, then at length I would slowly return home tacitae per amica silentia lunae.

In summer, hid from day's garish eye by the umbrage of trees, reclined at my length lentus in umbra, or seeking the lake to cool my fervid limbs.

While no care beyond today embittered my life, but jocund I enjoyed pleasure which I shall ever remember. But alas! I must leave you, time with swift wing approaches, I shall not see another spring, but oh fields still be you blest, may science ever flourish & you my companions pursue with ardour the course of science, & may not Phoebus refuse

117

coronas for your brows, & you little ones let no vice stain your present innocence.

For me, whithersoever the stream of life may carry me, wheresoever or whatsoever I be, I will still remember you, and even ~~when~~ ^{till} death's cold hand chills my vital faculties, H. shall never be erased from my heart dum memor ipse mei.

NOTES

I. TO THE NOTEBOOK

Page 1

W) Preceded by 'U' in the upper left-hand and 'V' in the upper right-hand corners of the front inside cover and followed by 'N' on Np. 3, 'O' on Np. 5, and 'S' on Np. 19.

His armour glittered) The first of the very early entries by W. W.; for the others see the first entries on Npp. 5, 11, 13, and 19. Was the missing word at the end of the first line 'moon'?

Aug 22 1749) The date of the storm referred to in the following entry and apparently pencilled in later.

Storm at Legberthwaite) The same storm as the St. John's water-spout referred to on Np. 4 and one long famous in the Lake district. Clarke gives a lengthy account of it in the *Survey* (p. 57); and No. 42 in Wilkinson's *Select Views in Cumberland, Westmoreland, and Lancashire* (London, 1810), in which the earliest printed form of W. W.'s *Guide to the Lakes* appeared as the letterpress, is entitled 'Legberthwaite Mill, St. John's Vale, taken after much rain'. See also West's *Guide*, p. 140; Gilpin's *Observations*, ii. 36–37; and William Hutchinson, *Excursion to the Lakes* (London, 1776), pp. 122–5. Christopher apparently looked on this storm as a Lake district counterpart of Virgil's destructive autumn storm in *Georgics*, i. 316–22.

Description of a sail upon Windermere by day) It was a nice contention among devotees of Lake district scenery whether a given lake could be seen to better advantage from points along the shore or from the water and whether day or night views were superior. Windermere was as commonly described during the day as Derwentwater was at night. One reason for such distinctions was that after the initial raptures of Dr. John Brown, who found the beauties of Rosa, Poussin, and Claude all exhibited at Keswick, each lake was supposed to have its own character. Thus Hutchinson tells us that 'the paintings of

119

Poussin describe the nobleness of Uls-water; the works of Salvator Rosa express the romantic and rocky scenes of Keswick; and the tender and elegant touches of Claude Lorrain and Smith pencil forth the rich variety of Windermere' (*Excursion*, p. 191). For descriptions of sails on Windermere by day see Gilpin, i. 151–9; Clarke, pp. 133–40, and Hutchinson, pp. 186–91.

on Derwent by night) Though Brown and Gray, who made a night piece on Derwentwater almost a requirement of a Lake writer, envisaged an evening walk, it was easy to translate their descriptions to a sail, as Hutchinson's account shows (see *Excursion*, pp. 165–6). The passage is also worth looking at because its tracing of the ascent of the moon shows how completely W. W. was working in a contemporary manner in *E.W.*

Page 2

In praise of the north) Cf. the Latin entry on L1v.

Let no one travel to see the boasted Alps) Cf. *Georgics*, ii. 136–76, and West, pp. 4–5.

hospitality reigns here) Cf. Npp. 4 and 15 and the picture of rural hospitality in *Excur.* v. 749–77. The hospitality of the dalesmen was a recurrent feature of the mountain-valley idyl.

Rydale particular) Cf. W. W.'s description of Rydal Falls in *E.W.*, ll. 71–84, and cf. this with Thomson's description of a cataract as given in Knox's *Elegant Extracts*, p. 225, referred to on L1v.

when read the Georgics) See also L1v. Like so many other eighteenth-century writers, Christopher looked to the *Georgics* as a principal model (cf. Dwight L. Durling, *The Georgic Tradition in English Poetry*, New York, 1935). W. W. also had a high regard for it. About 1789–90 he made two translations from it (*Poet. Wks.* i. 283, 285). *D.S.* was prefaced by epigraphs from the *Georgics* and Lucretius, the two classical sources directly referred to in the notebook, and ll. 636–43 are an elaboration of *Georgics*, iii. 66–68. It is extraordinary to observe the number of thematic relationships between Virgil's poem, the notebook, and W. W.'s poems. Virgil's fine apostrophe to the happy husbandman (ii. 458–74) would appear to underlie the entry on Np. 4 calling for 'praise of an husbandman's and shepherds life', and a good part of *Prel.* viii, a book rich in Virgilean allusions, is a development of W. W.'s highly individual version of this theme. Also, the very comparative development of the theme in this book, with its allusions to the 'smooth life' which shepherds of old time had by Virgilean rivers, is itself Virgilean (cf. *Georgics*, ii. 136–

76); and W. W.'s allusion to the sacrificial herds of Clitumnus (viii. 315–18) is a direct reference to ii. 145–8 in Virgil's own development of the comparative theme. It was also easy for eighteenth-century Englishmen contemplating the life of the dalesmen to see in their fairs and 'merry nights' counterparts of Virgil's festivals, country festivities, and contests of strength and endurance (*Georgics*, ii. 385–96, 527–31, and iii. 103–12). Thus Clarke tells us in the *Survey* (p. xxi) that 'the Sunday fairs and sports which are still kept up in England, and particularly in Cumberland, remind one also of the games usual at the solemn times and religious festivals of the ancients'. Cf. *Prel.* iv. 316–27 and viii. 1–61; *Excur.* ii. 115–46; and *The Waggoner*, ii. 30 ff. Other Georgical themes common to the notebook and W. W. include the destructive autumn storm (see above, pp. 59–60); armies in the sky (see above, pp. 29–32); and the mother bird mourning for her robbed nest (*Georgics*, iv. 511–15; Np. 18, and W. W., *Poet. Wks.* i. 284).

Hawkshead. School. Praise of lerning) Cf. W. W.'s first poem 'Lines Written as a School Exercise at Hawkshead', composed 1785–6.

Windermere. Echo.) The echo from Longholme Island is described by Gilpin (*Observations*, ii. 60), and Nicholas and Burn, *History and Antiquities of the Counties of Westmorland and Cumberland* (London, 1777, 2 vols.), i. 186.

to inquire of Mrs. T. about this) Mrs. Anne Tyson, the widow in whose house W. W. lodged as a schoolboy at Hawkshead. She is mentioned in *Prel.* viii. 220, as a source of tales of local tragedies, hazards, and escapes.

Rydal Lowdore) Cf. *E.W.*, ll. 5–6.

King of Patterdale) The richest statesman of the region, idealized by Gilpin (*Observations*, ii. 67), but denounced by Joseph Budworth, *A Fortnight's Ramble to the Lakes* (London, 1795, 2nd ed.), pp. 82, 90, 102, and 106, as a drunkard and miser. Cf. D. W. to Lady Beaumont in 1805 (*E.L.*, p. 538).

Read Guide to the Lakes) Thomas West's *Guide to the Lakes: Dedicated to Lovers of Landscape Studies*, first published in 1778 and thereafter in many editions, was the most famous of the early Lake district guidebooks. W. W. refers to it as having been popular for nearly fifty years (*Prose Wks.* ii. 100). All references in the present work are to the edition of 1789, the one cited in the notebook. West, a true devotee of picturesque travel, was an Ulverston resident who 'frequently accompanied genteel parties on a Tour of the Lakes'.

Gay's & Dr Browns Letters) In spite of an omitted 'r', clearly a reference to Gray's *Journal of His Northern Tour, in a Letter to Dr.*

Wharton and to Dr. John Brown's *Letter describing the Vale and Lake of Keswick*. Both are printed in the elaborate Addenda in the 1789 and most other editions of West's *Guide*; page references to the *Journal* in the notebook are regularly to this Addenda. In his own *Guide to the Lakes* W. W. wrote: 'Dr. Brown, the celebrated author of the *Estimate* . . . published a letter to a friend, in which the attractions of the Vale of Keswick were delineated with a powerful pencil, and the feeling of a genuine Enthusiast. Gray, the Poet, followed: he died soon after his forlorn and melancholy pilgrimage to the vale of Keswick, and the record left behind him of what he had seen and felt in his journey excited the pensive interest with which the human mind is ever disposed to listen to the farewell words of a man of genius. . . . Every reader of this journal must have been impressed with the words which conclude his notice of the vale of Grasmere' (*Prose Wks.* ii. 64). In 1794, while she was at Windy Brow with William and he was revising *E.W.*, Dorothy wrote a letter which contains a patent imitation of the Borrowdale idyl as given in Gray's *Journal* (*E.L.*, pp. 111–12).

Call-garth) Old Calgarth Hall on the eastern shore of Windermere, once the manor house of the Philipsons and now a farm house; not to be confused with the nearby 'new house' built by Bishop Watson of Llandaff and now a hospital. Cf. the entry on L3r., calling for a 'digression, at Call-garth' on superstition, and the cognate passage in W. W.'s *The Vale of Esthwaite* (see above, pp. 20–21). Obviously, Christopher regarded Calgarth and the superstitions connected with it (see Npp. 3, 13–14) as affording materials for developing the theme of local superstition which he associated with several of his chief models—'L'Allegro' (Np. 3), *The Seasons* (L3r.), and Collins's *Ode* (Npp. 13, L1v., and L3r.). Cf. the remarks on Lake district superstitions in Clarke's *Survey*, p. 56, and Budworth's *Fortnight's Ramble*, p. 126.

Description of robbing an eagle's nest) The reference is to Gray's account in the *Journal* as printed in West's *Guide* of an exploit of his young farmer of Borrowdale; it established the theme in Lake district literature (see Budworth's imitation in *Windermere. A Poem*, pp. 25–26), and cf. W. W.'s account of the robbing of ravens' nests in *Prel.* i. 333–50.

Page 3

Fairies are frequent here) Cf. W. W.'s fairy lore in *E.W.*, ll. 339–58; *The Triad* (ll. 170–3); 'Song at the Feast of Brougham Castle', ll. 128–33; 'The Wishing Gate'; 'The Faery Chasm'; *The River Duddon*, No. XI; *The Waggoner*, iv. 28–35; and 'The Seven Sisters'.

They are often seen sunning) Apparently a reference to mine fairies associated with the mining operations started in Patterdale in the eighteenth century (see Clarke, *Survey*, p. 35). Cf. *Comus*: 'No goblin, or swart Faery of the mine' (l. 435).

Their dances, etc) Cf. the references to *Midsummer Night's Dream* on Npp. 11 and 16; Beattie's *Minstrel*, I. xxxv; and W. W.'s 'The Faery Chasm' and *The Waggoner*, iv. 28–35.

They frequently spin for the maids) See above, p. 63.

In Patterdale a man used always to say) A patent case of localization of a widespread folklore theme. Cf. 'The Fairy Queen' in Percy's *Reliques*, ed. Prichard, ii. 252, and 'The Fairies' Farewell', p. 254.

Milton's l'allegro) The reference is especially to ll. 94–114, in which, if we take the reading of the 1645 edition, male and female rustics match each other with superstitious tales. Note that the same device is used in some ultimately rejected lines in *Guilt and Sorrow* in which the Female Vagrant equals the superstitions of the Sailor:

> Much of the wonders of that boundless heath
> He told. . . .
> Much more, of dreams from ancient ages fetch'd,
> And spectral sights that fill the shadowy plain
> . . . .
> *She told.*
>
> (*Poet. Wks.* i. 104–5)

Description of a Keswick Regatta) According to West, regattas came into fashion in the Lake district about 1780. They were held regularly on Derwentwater between 1781 and 1791 and at various times thereafter. Clarke (*Survey*, pp. 64–65) gives an extended account of one of them. W. W. alludes to a Windermere regatta in the 1850 *Prelude*:

> Once, when those summer months
> Were flown, and autumn brought its annual show
> Of oars with oars contending, sails with sails,
> Upon Winander's spacious breast, it chanced *etc.*
>
> (iv. 370–4)

Callgarth) Another reference to Old Calgarth Hall.

the sculls lie in a window) The window and room still exist, but the panelling has been removed. For the story connected with the skulls see Npp. 13–14 and the notes to those pages.

The Bp. has planted near his new house) The three lines on the bishop break the continuity between the preceding and following entries and appear to have been added after them. Richard Watson, Bishop of Llandaff, to whose strictures on the French Revolution

W. W. replied in 1793 with his *Letter to the Bishop of Llandaff*, inherited a large sum of money from a former pupil, purchased the Calgarth estate in the 1780's, and retired there toward the end of the decade. The foundations of his 'new house', to be distinguished from nearby Old Calgarth Hall, were laid in the summer of 1789. On the trees see above, pp. 11–12. For W. W.'s later relations with the bishop and his family see *M.Y.*, pp. 575, 613; *L.Y.*, pp. 50, 511; and *The Correspondence of Henry Crabb Robinson*, ed. Edith J. Morley (Oxford, 1927, 2 vols.), pp. 158, 485.

mentis gratissimus error) Horace, *Epis.* II. ii. 140. Christopher apparently wrote on top of the following English entry at once as he thought of this neat ending for one of his hexameters. Cf. *Prel.* vi. 105–12:

> In fine,
> I was a better judge of thoughts than words,
> Misled in estimating words, not only
> By common inexperience of youth,
> But by the trade in classic niceties,
> The dangerous craft of culling term and phrase
> From languages that want the living voice
> To carry meaning to the natural heart.

This error of Fancy was once frequent) The theme appears also in W. W.'s earliest poem 'Lines Written as a School Exercise at Hawkshead'.

Page 4

Description of the mists) On the relation of Beattie's description of mist in *The Minstrel* (I. xxi) to W. W. see above, pp. 45–46. It is doubtless impossible to tell which of Gilpin's various passages on mist Christopher had in mind, but in connexion with W. W. one can hardly fail to notice the following one:

The moisture and vapoury heaviness of our atmosphere, which produces the rich verdure of our lawns, gives birth also to another peculiar feature in English landscape—that obscurity which is often thrown over distance. In warmer climates especially, the air is purer. . . . Under Italian skies very remote objects are seen with great distinctness. . . .

The several degrees of obscurity, which the heaviness of our atmosphere gives to landscape, may be reduced to three—haziness, mists, and fogs.

Haziness just adds that light, gray tint—that thin, dubious veil, which is often beautifully spread over landscape. It hides nothing. It only sweetens the hues of nature—it gives a consequence to every common object, by giving it a more indistinct form—it corrects the glare of colours—it softens the harshness of lines; and above all, it throws over the face of landscape that harmonizing tint, which blends the whole into unity and repose.

Mist goes farther. It spreads still more obscurity over the face of nature, as haziness softens, and adds a beauty perhaps to the most correct forms of landscape; mist is adapted to those landscapes in which we want to hide much; to soften more; and to throw many parts into a greater distance than they naturally occupy.

Even the *fog*, which is the highest degree of a gross atmosphere, is not without its beauty in landscape, especially in mountain scenes. . . . When some vast promontory issuing from a cloud of vapour, with which all its upper parts are blended, shoots into a lake, the imagination is left at a loss to discover whence it comes, or to what height it aspires. The effect rises with the obscurity and the view is sometimes wonderfully great.

(*Observations*, i. 10–13)

Clarke writes in a similar fashion in the *Survey* (p. xxxv), and so does W. W. himself in the *Guide to the Lakes* (*Prose Wks*. ii. 43–45). Note the extraordinary relationship between the ideas held about mists and the views of W. W. and Coleridge on the imagination. Gilpin says that haziness (1) transforms and gives a consequence to every common object, and (2) that it blends multiplicity into unity. Cf. W. W.'s remarks in the Preface to the *Lyrical Ballads* about throwing over 'common objects a certain colouring of the imagination whereby ordinary things should be presented to the mind in an unusual aspect' and Coleridge's views on the unifying powers of the poetic imagination. W. W. himself makes the analogy explicit in his remarks on 'The Thorn': 'Arose out of my observing . . . on a stormy day, a thorn which I had often passed, in calm and bright weather, without noticing it. I said to myself, "Cannot I by some invention do as much to make this thorn permanently an impressive object as the storm has made it to my eyes at this moment?"' Hazlitt made exactly the right comment when he wrote of *The Excursion*: 'Every object is seen through the medium of innumerable recollections, and clothed with the haze of imagination, like a glittering vapour.' Cf. also Coleridge, *Biog. Lit.*, ed. Shawcross, ii. 5.

Gilpine) Cf. Np. 17. William Gilpin, the leading exponent of picturesque travel, published numerous accounts of his tours between 1782 and 1809 under the general title of *Observations relative to Picturesque Beauty*. W. W. refers to him in the note to l. 317 of *E.W.*, and mentions him in 1796 and 1798 (*E.L.*, pp. 155, 198). In *Prel.* xii. 106 f., 144–5, 154–6, and 185–9, the vogue for the picturesque is condemned and the impression is given that his own addiction to it was a passing aberration of the period of his disillusion in the French Revolution, presumably about 1795. It is evident, however, that he was under picturesque influences earlier than this date, that there were periodic later recrudescences of them, and that they were of greater importance than is sometimes supposed. Even when he was writing *The Prelude* itself, he was capable of remarking of a river scene that whatever Salvator could desire would there be found (*E.L.*, p. 365). It is clear, too, that as the sense of the visionary gleam faded away, Wordsworth returned to some degree to the conception of nature as scenery and picture. For all that he affects in the *Guide* to disdain viewing nature in this manner, that work was published in its first form as the letterpress accompanying a series of plates of Lake district scenery by Joseph Wilkinson, quotes Gilpin, and engages here and there in the manner of the picturesque writers in pointing out spots for the artist (*Prose Wks.* ii. 18). See further the preceding note. In his notes to *The River Duddon* he quotes from Green a long passage containing among other things a description of the picturesque conception of a 'station', or vantage point for viewing a scene, as a position 'elevated enough to show the various objects in the valley, and not so high as to diminish their importance' (*Poet. Wks.* iii. 509). Some years earlier he had himself embodied this conception in *The Recluse* when in the opening description he speaks of himself as having first seen the vale of Grasmere from a 'Station . . . not giddy yet aerial' (ll. 19–20).

Beatties Mins) Cf. L1r. Few poems sum up more completely the sentimental and melancholy themes of eighteenth-century poetry than *The Minstrel* of James Beattie, published in 1771 (part ii in 1774). Common to it and Christopher's entries are mists, storms and night scenes, echoes, ruminations on superstition and knowledge, praise of the spare shepherd life, legends and tales of fairy lore told on winter evenings, secluded vales, deer, pensive musings on the transitoriness of human joys, tales of rural tragedies, and a vision involving soldiers. Granted that these themes were all extremely common in late eighteenth-century poetry, it is still evident from the notebook that Beattie's was a major influence on Christopher's plans. The influence of that poet on W. W. has often been noted, attention to it having been directed by Wordsworth's own note to l. 116 of *E.W.* Not only does a kinship exist between the themes of the two, but it seemed to Dorothy that her brother William was such a poet as Beattie described. Writing to Jane Pollard on 10 July 1793, when she had not seen William for two years and a half, so that the impression takes us back to the end of 1790 or the beginning of 1791, she quotes a line from *The Minstrel* and continues: 'That verse of Beattie's *Minstrel* always reminds me of him, and indeed the whole character of Edwin resembles much what William was when I first knew him—after my leaving Halifax—"and oft he traced the uplands" etc. etc. etc.' (*E.L.*, pp. 97–98). The resemblance, moreover, struck not only Dorothy but William himself. In a letter to Mathews in 1795 he described his own activities by quoting from *The Minstrel* (*L.Y.* iii. 1334). Moreover, in 1802 in 'Stanzas Written in My Pocket Copy of Thomson's *Castle of Indolence*', he draws a portrait of himself the resemblance of which to Beattie's minstrel has more than once been remarked.

No banditti haunt the mountains) 'No villainous banditti haunt

126

the mountains; innocent people live in the dells. Every cottager is narrative of all he knows; and mountain virtue and pastoral hospitality are found at every farm' (West, *Guide to the Lakes,* p. 135). It should also be noted that banditti belong in the picturesque tradition. Gilpin, for example, says: 'With regard to the adorning of such a landscape with figures, nothing could suit it better than a group of banditti' (*Observations,* i. 174). On the hospitality of the dalesmen see also the first entry on Np. 2 and above, pp. 68–69.

Borrowdale) The beautiful valley south of Derwentwater which figures prominently in what I have called the mountain-valley idyl. Cf. Np. 15 and L3*v.,* and see above, pp. 67–71.

praise of a husbandman's & shepherds life) Page 431 of Knox's *Elegant Extracts of Poetry* contains under the title 'The Blessings of a Shepherd's Life' the beginning of Henry's speech in *3 Henry VI,* ii. v. 21–54.

Elegant Extracts) 'In a bulky volume of Poetry entitled *Elegant Extracts in Verse,* which must be known to most of my Readers, as it is circulated everywhere and in fact constitutes at this day the poetical library of our Schools' &c. (W. W., *Prose Wks.* iii. 176). The work referred to is *Elegant Extracts, or Useful and Entertaining Pieces of Poetry,* compiled by Vicesimus Knox.

Begin the day with thanks to God) Cf. Thomson, 'Autumn', ll. 151–76, a passage which occurs on p. 357 of *Elegant Extracts,* one of the pages of that work specifically singled out on L1*v.* (see '356 etc'). It also doubtless reflects *P.L.* v. 136 ff., the passage in which occurs Adam's and Eve's 'morning hymn' (see the reference to these lines on Np. 11 and above, pp. 60–62, for reflections of them in W. W.'s poems).

& go to work with the song of the lark) Cf. *Prel.* iv. 338–9:

> Dews, vapours, and the melody of birds,
> And Labourers going forth into the fields.

A description of the waterspout) Cf. the reference on Np. 1 to the storm at Legberthwaite, the same one as the St. John's storm of 1749. On the page cited in the *Guide to the Lakes,* West gives an extended account of this memorable storm, during which torrential rains pouring down the mountains to the east brought down huge stones from them and flooded the whole valley. In spite of the heavy rains that are characteristic of the Lake district, one would gather that it was the most destructive storm in years, and there are possibly echoes of it in the storm in Canto I of *The Waggoner,* which occurs farther down along a route leading into St. John's Vale, and in the remark in *The Brothers* that a Lake district waterspout could bring down half a mountain (ll. 131–51). See further above, pp. 59–60.

Description of the echoes produced by guns etc) See also Np. 5 and above, pp. 36–40. Cf. Gilpin: 'We took notice of a very grand echo on the western shores of the great island in Windermere; but the most celebrated echoes are said to be found on Ulleswater; in some of which the sound of a cannon is distinctly reverberated six, or seven times. . . . Such a variety of awful sounds, mixing and commixing, and at the same moment heard from all sides, have a wonderful effect on the mind; as if the very foundations of every rock on the lake were giving away; and the whole scene, from some strange convulsion, were falling into general ruin' (*Observations*, ii. 60–62).

Coniston) There may have been guns for producing echoes on Coniston Water, as on the other lakes, but if so contemporary descriptions appear to make no mention of them. The echoes for which this region was noted were rather those from the blasting and other activities of quarries (see, for example, the description of them by W. W.'s schoolfellow and college friend Charles Farish in *The Minstrels of Winandermere*, 1811, p. 15). W. W. was probably thinking of the Coniston quarries and their echoes in *E.W.*, ll. 140–6, and the following lines are found in MS. A of *The Prelude*:

> The quarry man whose thunders all day long
> Break forth at intervals and chase the sleep
> Of Echo. She is ris'n and hurries round
> And round the amplest circuit of the hills.
>> (*Prel.*, p. 287)

All that remains of this in the 1805–6 text is viii. 503:

> The Quarry-man far heard! that blasts the rock,

and even this disappears in the final version.

Page 5

his crest nodded dreadful) The second in the series of very early entries by W. W. (see above, pp. 3–10). The notation appears to echo *P.L.* iv. 985–9:

> On the other side Satan allarm'd
> Collecting all his might dilated stood,
> Like Teneriff or Atlas unremoved:
> His stature reached the Skie, and on his Crest
> Sat horror Plum'd.

Cf. in the revisions of the passage on the cock in *E.W.*:

> Long glittering plumes his gorgeous form o'erspread
> A crest embattled tops his warrior head.
>> (*Poet. Wks.* i. 17)

Description of the crags that fell at Lowdore banks) Gray's description is possibly echoed in one of the 1794 revisions of *E.W.* (see *Poet. Wks.* i. 18).

Description of an evening) The page cited in West contains Gray's description of his evening walk at Keswick. See above, p. 41.

Guns & Music for Echo) Cf. Np. 4 and the notes to that page and see above, pp. 36–40.

Page 6

The vigour activity & strength of the youth) Cf. L3*r.*, and the account of Oswald in *Excur.* vii. 739–857.

They climb the rock in search of the lamb) Assuredly an actual activity of shepherds but also a literary motif. Cf. Dyer's *The Fleece*:

> Huge Breaden's stony summit once I climb'd
> After a kidling.

A selection containing this passage appears in *Elegant Extracts* on p. 221, one of the pages referred to on Ll*v.* Cf. *Prel.* viii. 221–310.

Their exercises) Cf. L3*r.* Clarke says: 'On the 10th of July the neighbouring shepherds assemble here [Patterdale] and hold a festival, during which there are horse races, wrestling, and other such like country diversions . . . they also at this time amuse themselves with fox-hunting' (*Survey*, p. 41). Cf. the Helvellyn fair in *Prel.* viii. 1–61, and the rustic May-day festival in *Excur.* ii. 144–5.

running) Cf. *Excur.* ii. 144–5:

> By the fleet racers, ere the sun be set,
> The turf of yon large pasture will be skimmed.

wrestling) Cf. *Excur.* ii. 146:

> There, too, the lusty wrestlers shall contend.

dancing) Cf. *Prel.* iv. 316–27; *D.S.*, ll. 41–42; and the village 'merry night' in *The Waggoner*, ii. 30 ff., esp. 51–69.

Female beauty) Cf. Hutchinson: 'The women of this country are remarkably beautiful;—the bold unintelligent stare, the fluttering inconsistent pertness, and lisping nonsense, too much characteristic of the sex in some northern countries, are here totally discarded, and in their room are substituted intelligent looks clothed with modesty, and politeness united with simplicity of manners' (*Excursion to the Lakes*, p. 119).

Hunting the fox. red deer etc.) D. W. refers in her *Journals* to an annual red deer hunt in Martindale (i. 416), apparently the same one described by Clarke in the *Survey* (p. 34). Some such hunt is referred to in *Excur*. vii. 861–5:

> One day—a summer's day of annual pomp
> And solemn chase—from morn to sultry noon
> His steps had followed, fleetest of the fleet,
> The red deer driven along his native heights
> With cry of hound and horn.

Daffodils early in the spring) See above, pp. 65–66.

G. Park. Deer) Gowbarrow Park, a tract of about 2,000 acres bordering on Ullswater, was proclaimed a forest by William Rufus, but the oaks in which it once abounded had been largely cut down by the latter part of the eighteenth century. Hutchinson says that it had six or seven hundred head of fallow deer (*History of Cumberland*, i. 435).

To Derwent) Inverted in erased pencil and hard to read. Cf. L3*v*.

Page 7

In autumn misty evening) See above, pp. 16–17.

Ask Leeson. Yes. Atkinson) Probably schoolfellows of Christopher. See above, p. 12.

In the spring morning) Cf. *The Seasons*, 'Spring', ll. 597–607, in which the lark, thrush, and blackbird appear in the same order.

Page 8

I dwell with delight) See above, pp. 56–57.

How different are the busy) Cf. *E.W.* 13 ff., and some rejected lines in MS. I of *Guilt and Sorrow* (*Poet. Wks.* i. 105).

Page 9

glead) Northern for *glede*, the kite.

West's 1st station) See above, p. 22.

West's secd.) Not West's second Windermere station, which called for a view from the south side of the Great Island, but the view from near-by Harrow which West gives as an alternative to his first station. Apparently Christopher preferred a slightly different position.

Belle Grange) North of the ferry on the west side of Windermere.

Brother's Water) Clarke, referred to in the immediately following entry, says: 'In Broadwater, or Brotherwater, two young men
(brothers) were drowned together in December, 1785, by the ice
breaking with them. The inhabitants have a tradition that it received
its name of Brotherwater from the like circumstance happening once
before' (*Survey*, pp. 153–4). Dorothy tells the story (*Journals*, i. 418–
19), and William gives a briefer version of it in his *Guide to the Lakes*
(*Prose Wks.* ii. 113). Cf. *Prel.* viii. 229–31:

> they look'd down
> On Deep-dale Head, and Brothers-water, named
> For those two Brothers that were drown'd therein.

Clarke recommends) Cf. Np. 12. James Clarke brought out his
Survey of the Lakes of Cumberland, Westmorland, and Lancashire
in 1787, and the work had a second edition in 1789. Though a sur-
veyor, Clarke also undertook to give historical and descriptive
accounts of the region and for all his affected disdain for the picturesque writers, was himself an assiduous describer of stations for
viewing scenery. W. W. refers to this work in his note to l. 187 of *An
Evening Walk*. It contains extensive accounts of the lawless condi-
tions which prevailed among the 'borderers' in former times which
may well lie in the background of Wordsworth's play.

Butterlip How) The conical hill, from a station half-way up which
Clarke declared that the finest view of the Vale of Grasmere was to
be had (*Survey*, p. 120). It was the favourite goal of the walks of
William and Dorothy from Dove Cottage and is referred to repeatedly
in the *Grasmere Journal*. From the persistence with which she mentions it (pp. 62, 78, 82, &c.), it is likely that it constituted what she
refers to as the 'grand view' of the valley.

Slape Crag) On the western side of the middle part of Windermere
and recommended as a vantage point for viewing the lake by Clarke
(*Survey*, p. 142).

Summer the ceaseless hum of insects) Cf. Thomson, 'Summer',
ll. 282–3:

> Nor undelightful is the ceaseless hum
> To him who muses through the woods at noon.

At the beginning of autumn) Cf. the related entry on Np. 16. The
notation fuses the St. John's storm of 1749 (see Npp. 1 and 4) with
recollections of Virgil, *Aeneid*, x. 802–8, a favourite passage with
W. W., and one reflected in the 1794 revisions of *An Evening Walk*
(*Poet. Wks.* i. 21).

Thus in life a sudden storm) Virgilian moralizing quite in the manner of the age and of *E.W.*, l. 361, and *D.S.*, l. 636.

Page 11

Mighty was the warr[ior?]) The third in the series of very early entries by W. W. See above, pp. 3–10.

Evening. Night. Elegant Extracts . . . Mid. Nights Dream) Cf. Np. 16. Page 387 contains *Midsummer Night's Dream*, v. 378–97. The opposite page contains the famous lines on the poetic imagination (v. 12–17), which are echoed in the revisions which W. W. made in *E.W.*, in 1794 (see *Poet. Wks.* i. 13). Page 383 of *Elegant Extracts* contains the passage in which Lorenzo and Jessica call the roll of great lovers (*Merchant of Venice*, v. 1–22).

Could not I introduce an Hymn) Cf. Np. 18. Thomson's 'Hymn on the Seasons' begins on p. 4 of *Elegant Extracts*, one of the pages referred to on L1v. Milton's 'Morning Hymn' of Adam and Eve, based on Psalm 148 (*P.L.* v. 153–208) opens Knox's collection. The theme was a common one. Cf. Ogilvie's 'Hymn from Psalm 148' in *Elegant Extracts*, p. 4. For the influence of Milton's lines on W. W. see above, pp. 60–62.

Page 12

Stations) A term associated with the cult of the picturesque and denoting not merely a vantage point for the viewing of scenery but a point from which a picture-like view was presented or the Claude glass which Gray had made fashionable could be effectively used. Stations in this sense are regularly recommended in West's *Guide* and similar works. It is significant of the persistence of the influence of certain phases of the picturesque on W. W. that he used the term both early and late (see *Recl.*, l. 19; *Prose Wks.* ii. 6; 'Black Comb', l. 13; the Fenwick note to 'Lines Left upon a Seat in a Yew Tree'; and his note to *The River Duddon*. It was believed that the ideal station was a point above the scene to be viewed but not too far above it (see on this point 'Gilpine' in the notes to Np. 4). The fame of Butterlip How as a station for viewing the vale of Grasmere rested partly on the exactness with which the path around it and half way up met this requirement.

Windermere. Hill above the ferry) Cf. Np. 9 and note. Identical with West's first station for viewing Windermere and a favourite spot with W. W. when he was a Hawkshead schoolboy; referred to by him with an allusion to West in the Fenwick note to 'Lines Left upon a Seat in a Yew Tree'.

Near Harrowslack) Cf. Np. 9 and note.

South end of the Great Island) West's second Windermere station.

North end of Id.) West's No. III.

Rawlinson's Nab) West's No. IV.

Hill above Bowness) West's No. V, but both West (pp. 67–70) and Clarke (*Survey*, pp. 141–2) quote Arthur Young's earlier description of the scene. The view from this point is apparently also the one described at the opening of Book IV of *The Prelude*.

A little behind Rayrigg) Recommended by West, pp. 74–75.

Near Rydal Hall) The view from a spot 'near Rydal Hall' was one of Clarke's recommendations (*Survey*, p. 125).

Clarke recommends Butterlip How) See Np. 10 and note.

Pages 55, 56, 57, 16, 134, 136) Notations in soft pencil partly written over by the later entries in ink. They clearly refer to Clarke's *Survey*. Pages 55–56 contain the account of the spectral horsemen of Southerfell, referred to by Christopher on Np. 14 and used by W. W. in *An Evening Walk*; p. 57 gives an account of the waterspout at Legberthwaite on 22 August 1749, mentioned on Npp. 1 and 4; p. 134 contains a reference to the Calgarth skulls referred to on Npp. 3, 13–14; and p. 136 contains the concluding part of a wretched poem on the taming of a shrew and an account of the Cork Lad of Kentmere, a poor boy of prodigious strength (cf. the first entry on Np. 6). Page 16 contains an account of the exhuming of the Giant's Grave in the Penrith churchyard. For the relation of this to a passage in one of the revisions of *An Evening Walk* see above, pp. 33–34.

Slape Crag) See Np. 10 and note.

Grasmere Farington Opposite Helm Crag) Joseph Farington published two series of engravings of the Lake district, an early one of twenty plates and another of forty-three in 1816. Individual plates in the first series in some cases bear dates earlier than 1789, but they were apparently not collected in a published edition until 1789. They are 'proposed' in the third (1784) edition of West's *Guide* and advertised in the fourth edition of 1789.

D° Windermere Gill Head) No. 14 in Farington's first series is a 'View of Windermere-water from Gill Head, below Bowness'.

D° Directly opposite Bowness) Farington's No. 17 is a 'View across Windermere-water, looking over the great island, from the hill above the ferry house'.

D° Above Ra[y]rig, looking down) Farington's No. 19.

Dᵒ Legberthwaite 6th milestone) Farington's No. 18; referred to also by West, *Guide*, p. 84.

A few yards out of the road before you come to the bridge) The bridge referred to in this entry was probably that over the Emont. Clarke says: 'Emont Bridge divides Cumberland and Westmorland. . . . From the middle arch is a beautiful view either side up or down the river, and perhaps few places are better disposed in point of picturesque beauty, though none have been less noticed' (*Survey*, p. 11). The surrounding area was the scene of many of W. W.'s rambles during his college vacations when he tells us that he went in quest of 'works of art' and 'scenes renowned for beauty' (*Prel.*, 1850, vi. 190–223).

Page 13

his consort is sad) The fourth in the series of very early entries by W. W.

Two sculls) The Calgarth skulls. Cf. Np. 3 and see below.

A Farmer) A family of farmers occupied the habitable portion of Old Calgarth Hall in Christopher's day (West, *Guide*, p. 64). Though the story of spectral music is a widespread folklore motif, it does not occur in any of the printed accounts of the house. W. W. used the idea of supernatural sounds presaging the death of a maid in one of his boyhood poems, the 'Dirge Sung by a Minstrel'.

The sculls) West says: 'There are two human skulls, which have lain in the window of a large room as long as can be remembered, whose history and reputed properties are too singular not to contribute something to this story of *the haunted house*, and to let them pass over in this note.

'It has been a popular tale in these parts, of immemorial standing, that these skulls formerly belonged to two poor old people, who were unjustly executed for a robbery; that, to perpetuate their innocence, some ghost brought them there, and that they are for that end indestructible, and, in effect, *immovable*. For, it is said, to what place soever they were taken, or however used, they were still presently seen again in their old dormitory, the window. As the report goes, they have been buried, burnt, powdered, and dispersed to the wind, and upon the lake, several times to no purpose, as to their removal or destruction. So far says common fame. Certain it is that human remains still exist. And it would be thought an impeachment of the taste and curiosity of the nymphs and swains of the neighbouring villages, if they could not say that they had *once* seen the skulls of Callgarth. . . . But be their origin what it may, their legend is too whimsical and improbable to deserve being recorded, otherwise than as an instance of the never-failing credulity of ignorance and super-stition' (*Guide*, p. 66). Clarke says that the two old persons were murdered by Robin the Devil, a notorious seventeenth-century mem-ber of the Philipson family, that the skulls had been carried off to London and had not reappeared, and that the whole tale was a com-pound of ridiculous falsehoods (*Survey*, p. 134). The account in the notebook contains details obviously from neither source, nor are they from Gilpin, who says much about Robin the Devil but nothing about Calgarth. Probably local tradition was also drawn on. Rawnsley gives an account which identifies the unfortunate victims as Kraster and Dorothy Cook and the wicked magistrate as Myles Philipson. He also gives the curse: 'Guard thyself, Myles Philipson, thou mayest think thou hast managed grandly, but that tiny plot of garden ground will be the dearest ever bought. Time shall be that no Philipson shall own an acre, and while Calgarth walls shall stand, we shall haunt it night and day' (*Literary Associations of the English Lakes*, Glasgow, 1901, ii. 77). The tale of reappearing skulls, like that of supernatural music, is a widespread folklore motif.

[?] Collins) Very faintly written in pencil under the entries in ink and suggesting that Christopher viewed the story of the Calgarth skulls as such a northern superstition as Collins recommended. On L3*r*. Calgarth is specifically associated with the 'Ode on the Popular Superstitions of the Highlands of Scotland'. The ode was first pub-lished in 1788 and W. W.'s 'Remembrance of Collins' dates from the following year.

they put some silver spoons amongst it) Cf. Genesis xliv.

Page 14

One evening upon Southerfell) Southerfell is east of Skiddaw and northeast of Keswick. Clarke's account of the spectral horsemen associated with this place follows that of a 'Mr. Lancaster of Blake-hills': 'On the 23rd of June, 1744, his father's servant, Daniel Stricket . . . about half past seven in the evening was walking a little above the house. Looking round him, he saw a troop of men on horseback riding on Southerfell-side, (a place so steep that an horse can scarcely travel on it at all,) in pretty close ranks, and at a brisk walk. Stricket looked earnestly at them for some time before he durst venture to acquaint anyone with what he saw, as he had the year before made himself ridiculous by a visionary story, which I beg leave here also to relate: He was at that time servant to John Wren of Wiltonhill, the next house to Blakehills, and sitting one evening after supper at the door along with his master, they saw a man with a dog pursuing some horses along Southerfell-side; and they seemed to run at an amazing pace, till they got out of sight at the low end of the Fell. This made them resolved to go next morning to the place to pick up the shoes which they thought these horses must have lost in galloping at such a furious rate; they expected likewise to see prodigious grazes from the feet of these horses on the steep side of the mountain, and to find the man lying dead, as they were sure he run so fast that he must kill himself. Accordingly they went, but to their great surprise, found not a shoe, nor even a single vestige of any horse having been there, much less did they find the man lying dead as they expected. This story they sometime concealed; at length, however, they ventured to tell it, and were (as might be expected) heartily laughed at. Stricket, conscious of his former ridiculous error, observed these aerial troops some time before he ventured to mention what he saw: at length, fully satisfied that what he saw was real, he went into the house, and told Mr. Lancaster he had something curious to shew him. . . . They then went together, and before Stricket spoke or pointed to the place, Mr. Lancaster himself discovered the phenomenon and said to Stricket, "Is this what thou hast to shew me?" "Yes, Master", replied Stricket: "Do you think you see as I do?" They found they did see alike, so they went and alarmed the family, who all came, and all saw this strange phenomenon.

'These visionary horsemen seemed to come from the lowest part of Souther-Fell, and became visible first at a place called Knott; then they moved in regular troops along the side of the Fell, till they came opposite Blakehills, where they went over the mountain: thus they described a kind of curvilinear path upon the side of the Fell, and both their first and last appearance were bounded by the top of the mountain.

'Frequently the last, or last but one, in a troop (always either the one or the other) would leave his place, gallop to the front, and then take the same pace with the rest, a regular, swift walk: these changes happened to every troop, (for many troops appeared), and oftener than once or twice. . . . Nor was this wonderful phenomenon seen at Blakehills only, it was seen by every person at every cottage within the distance of a mile; neither was it confined to a momentary view. . . .

'Thus I have given the best account I can procure of this wonderful appearance; let others determine what it was. This country, like every other where cultivation has been lately introduced, abounds in the *aniles fabellae* of fairies, ghosts, and apparitions; but these are never even fabled to have been seen by more than one or two persons at a time, and the view is always said to be momentary. Speed tells indeed of something similar to this as preceding a dreadful intestine war. Can something of this nature have given rise to Ossian's grand and awful mythology? or, finally, Is there any impiety in supposing, as this happened immediately before that rebellion which was intended to subvert the liberty, law, and the religion of England; that though immediate prophecies have ceased, these visionary beings might be directed to warn mankind of approaching tumults? In short, it is difficult to say what it was, or what it was not' (*Survey*, pp. 55–56). For W. W.'s use of this tale in *An Evening Walk* and *The Prelude* see above, pp. 29–32, 54–55. William Hutchinson in his *History of Cumberland* (1794) puts the appearances on Midsummer Eves in 1735, 1737, and 1745, and declares that a similar vision of an army marching was seen in Leicestershire in 1707 (i. 419–21).

They were involved in a lawsuit) This and the following entry give an alternative version of the story of the Calgarth skulls on Np. 13. According to Clarke, the Philipsons remained in possession of Calgarth until 1714, when the family ended in daughters who sold the estate (*Survey*, p. 133).

Discite justitiam) *Aeneid*, vi. 620.

Even-handed justice) Cf. *Macbeth*, I. vii. 10–12:

> This even-handed justice
> Commends the ingredients of our poison'd chalice
> To our own lips.

Page 15

Mines) See above, p. 128.

Coniston C.) Thomas Pennant says of Coniston Fells that they formerly yielded copper, but that the mines had been neglected in recent years because of the poverty of the ore (*Tour of Scotland*, 1790, i. 34–35).

Newland Lead & C.) 'Here in a hill called Gold-scope, are the remains of a famous ancient copper-mine which exhibits some curious excavations' (West, *Guide*, pp. 128–9; also mentioned by Clarke in the *Survey*, p. 85).

Borrowdale Wad) 'The road continued good to Rosthwaite, the first village in this romantic region, where it divides. That on the right leads to the *wad*-mines, and to Ravenglass; that on the left, to Hawkshead' (West, *Guide*, pp. 97–98). See also Gilpin, *Observations*, i. 213. *Wad*, black lead (*O.E.D.*).

Pastoral life. Borrowdale) See above, pp. 67–68. The preceding entries appear to follow West, who proceeds in the *Guide* on p. 98, as do the notations at this point, from mines to pastoral life in the Borrowdale region.

Langdale) Cf. the scene of bucolic festivity in *Excur.* ii. 111–46. On the role of Langdale as a setting in this poem see the Fenwick note (*Poet. Wks.* v. 376).

Hospitality) Cf. Npp. 2 and 4.

Scale force) A description of this waterfall near the head of Crummock Water appeared in the first version of W. W.'s *Guide to the Lakes,* but was later omitted.

ascend Skiddaw or Grasmire) An entry suggestive of a descriptive passage on the view from a mountain top in the manner of Dyer's 'Grongar Hill' (cf. the entry 'Skiddaw. Grongar hill' on L3*r*.). Descriptions of the view from the top of Skiddaw were attempted by a number of late eighteenth-century writers, among them Mrs. Radcliffe, the Gothic novelist and admirer of the paintings of Salvator Rosa and Claude Lorrain, who made the ascent of the mountain in 1794 and whose 'Description of the Scenery in a Ride over Skiddaw' became a regular feature of the extensive Addenda in the later editions of West's *Guide.* See also Pennant, *Tour of Scotland,* i. 46; Hutchinson, *Excursion,* pp. 169–70; Arthur Young, *A Six Months' Tour through the North of England,* iii. 156; and Joseph Budworth's *A Fortnight's Ramble,* pp. 220–2.

As in life the ambitious) Moralizing in a common eighteenth-century vein. Cf. Goldsmith's Dedication to *The Traveller* and Thomson, 'Autumn', ll. 1297–1300.

Page 16

A Whirlwind in 1790) See above, pp. 59–60. A Lake district analogue of the classical whirlwind in the description of a storm by Lucretius referred to on L1*r*. Cf. also *Georgics,* i. 316–21, and Thomson, 'Autumn', ll. 311–50, which occur on one of the pages (126) of *The Seasons* referred to on L1*r*. Note the query on Np. 20 about whirlwinds or 'whirlblasts' and cf. W. W.'s lines 'A Whirlblast from behind the hill'.

Then oft (in Winter) the peasants at night) See above, p. 29.

Introduction concerning superstition.) Cf. Np. 2 and L3*r*. There is much about superstition in late eighteenth-century poetry, in writers on the Lake district, almost all of whom make it an outstanding characteristic of the region, and in the early poetry of W. W. The theme turns up in his earliest poem, the 'Lines Written as a School Exercise'.

Grasmere morning) Cf. Npp. 1 and 17.

Windermere Noon) Bk. IV of *The Prelude* opens with a description of Windermere at noon. Cf. Np. 1 and notes.

Derwent, Evening & Night) See above, pp. 40–41, and cf. Np. 1 and notes.

Ulswater. Storm) Gilpin, who saw Ullswater on a clear day, expressed the opinion that it would be magnificent in a storm and could not refrain from imagining what it would be like on such an occasion (*Observations*, ii. 58–59).

Evening. Night.) Cf. Np. 11.

Oft at the beginning of autumn) Cf. the similar entry on Np. 10 and note.

Page 17

Evening. The reflection of the mountains) A convention of eighteenth-century topographical poetry.

See Gilpin. Eu. Mag. Jan. 88) The *European Magazine* for January 1788 contains an extended review of Gilpin's Lake district *Observations* with extensive quotations. W. W.'s early sonnet 'On Seeing Miss Helen Maria Williams Weep' appeared in this magazine in the February 1787 issue.

After the descriptions of Morning Noon etc.) Cf. L1r. An attempt to combine the Miltonic and Thomsonian schemes of arrangement, but probably directly suggested by one of the extracts quoted in the review of Gilpin's *Observations* cited in the previous entry.

scaiting on Esthwaite. Addison's Latine poem) Cf. *Prel.* i. 452–89, and see above, pp. 53–54. Apparently Christopher had in mind the 'Cursus Glacialis', which was asserted to be Addison's in Curll's edition of 1725 and was included in the *Miscellaneous Works* of 1750. In *Musae Anglicanae*, it appeared under the signature of Philip Frowde. The following anonymous translation is printed in the Bohn edition of Addison's *Works*, vi. 585–7:

> See nature round a hoary prospect yields,
> And beds of snow conceal the whiten'd fields;
> Bleak winter blasts, congealing where they fly,
> Shoot their keen darts, and mingling fill the sky.
> The silent streams in murmurs cease to move,
> Locked in their shores by icy bonds above:
> No more through vales they draw their hardened train,
> But form unmoved, a silent, silver plain:
> The watery gods, who dwell in courts below,
> Lament their stubborn waves no longer flow;

Each sad to view the empire where he reigns,
Enclosed above, and bound with crystal chains.
    Yet this bleak season of th' inclement year
Can boast delights the smiling youth to cheer;
With vigorous sports the winter's rage defy,
New brace the nerves, and active life supply.
    Each now the labour hardy to endure,
Who boast a steady strength, and tread secure,
With panting joy the frozen kingdom gain,
Rush to the shore, and hide the crackling plain:
Now in long tracks with sailing speed they shoot,
And tire unarmed the vigour of the foot:
Now o'er the race in winding circles, wheel,
Drove round, and carried on their shining steel.
    See! where the youth with eager passion glow,
Bound from above, and fill the plains below;
Skim lightly o'er the waves and scarce deface
With beauteous prints the silver-shining race.
See! in the midst of their smooth journey, skilled,
They stop, and turn, and mark the glittering field;
Razing the surface, on they wheel around
Which bends, and yields, and cracks beneath the wound:
They o'er the chace with easy labour drove,
Now here, now there, in endless mazes move.
    If we such pleasures from its rigour gain,
The winter sheds its keenest rage in vain,
While with full joy the panting heart o'erflows,
And the fair cheek with fairer purple glows.
    Here, if by chance, unable to convey
Too great a weight, the parting ice give way;
Or the bright knots which on its surface rise,
O'erturn the hasty racer as he flies;
What shouts, what laughter, fill the echoing skies!
No pity in one merry face appears
The wretch o'erwhelmed with jokes instead of tears:
His treacherous feet, and garments, as they flow,
Augment his fellows' joy, the hero's woe.
    But if, descending on the slippery plain,
The rival youth for fame and glory strain;
Shoot from the barrier, and with wishful eye,
To reach the goal, bend forward as they fly:
Breathless, around their eager arms they throw,
And lend new swiftness to their feet below.
No even tracks confess their winding way,
Confused they cross and in meanders play;
Orb within orb, their sportive toil we view,
Whitening with steel the circles where they flew. . . .

Fired with the thought etc.) Cf. L1r.

Praise of learing etc. & Hawkshead) Cf. Np. 2, and W. W.'s
'Lines Written as a School Exercise at Hawkshead'.

Fishing) Cf. *Prel.* i. 509–16.

As slowly I wander by) There are few pages in the notebook on which Christopher sounds more like William than on this one. W. W. on one occasion carried his fondness for desultory wandering to the point of invoking the sun to 'mount slowly' that he might 'wander long' (*Excur.* ii. 111). Cf. *Prel.* iv. 375–7:

> On I went
> Tranquil, receiving in my own despite
> Amusement, as I slowly pass'd along.

In summer reclined under thy trees) Cf. *E.W.*, ll. 63–64:

> When schoolboys stretch'd their length upon the green
> And round the humming elm, a glimmering scene.

Oft Hd. have I heard) Hawkshead. Cf. Dyer's:

> And often by the murmuring rill,
> Hears the thrush, while all is still,
> Within the groves of Grongar Hill.

These lines are echoed by W. W. in the sonnet 'To the Poet, John Dyer':

> Long as the thrush shall pipe on Grongar Hill.

Dyer's poem is mentioned by Christopher on L3*r*., and Christopher's apparent plan for passages on the evening and morning songs of the lark has a counterpart in W. W.'s *Miscellaneous Sonnets*, Nos. XXXIV and XXXV, written in 1838.

it delighted me to lead my wildly devious way) See above, p. 15.

Along thy banks) The places referred to are Windermere, Coniston, Esthwaite, Grasmere, and Rydal Cascade.

I have often watched the sun setting) In the Fenwick note to 'Dear Native Regions' W. W. tells us that the image of the light of the setting sun lingering on eastern hills first suggested itself to him as a boy when he was in a boat on the western side of Coniston Water in the shade of a row of sycamores. Cf.:

> Once—while, in that shade
> Loitering, I watched the golden beams of light
> Flung from the setting sun, as they reposed
> In silent beauty on the naked ridge
> Of a high eastern hill.
> (*Prel.*, 1850, viii. 462–75)

Cf. also *The Vale of Esthwaite*, ll. 508–13. Readers of late eighteenth-century poetry will question whether the image was as original with him as he supposed. In this entry, however, it is not only the first image which is striking, but the whole succession of them to the end of the page and their relationship to the concluding 'night piece' of *An Evening Walk*, for which the entry sounds almost like a prose plan (cf. ll. 399–404, 423–4, 433–46).

Page 18

Description of a man perishing in the snow) L3*r*. contains a reference to p. 175 of Thomson's *Seasons*, which contains 'Winter', ll. 276–321. These lines, under the title 'Description of a Man Perishing in the Snow', also appear in *Elegant Extracts* on p. 356, a page mentioned on L1*v*. On their relation to *D.S.* see above, pp. 42–44, and cf. *Excur.* v. 736–75, and D. W.'s *Journals*, i. 418.

I have felt along thy banks) Certainly anticipatory of *The Prelude* in tone and manner, but also representing Christopher attempting an answer to his query on Np. 11 about imitating the hymns of Milton and Thomson. Cf. *V. of Es.*:

> Lone wandering oft by Esthwaite's s[tream]
> My soul has felt the mystic drea[m.]
> (ll. 75–76)

I counted in the long Room) At Calgarth?

Oft have I watched . . . but never plundered them) Reflects *Georgics*, iv. 511–15, in which, as W. W. translated them in 1788–9, as Orpheus mourns for Eurydice,

> So darkling in the poplar's shady gloom
> Mourns the lone nightingale her hapless doom;
> Mourns with low sighs and sadly pleasing tongue,
> Torn callow from their nest, her darling youth;
> All night she weeps, slow-pouring from her throat
> Renew'd at every fall the plaintive note,
> Moans round the cheerless nest with pious love;
> The solemn warblings sadden all the grove.

The passage stuck in Wordsworth's mind. After 1820 he recast his translation of it, and it is perhaps reflected in *Peter Bell*, ll. 649–50:

> Like a poor bird—her plundered nest distrest
> Hovering around with dolorous moan.

Earlier, Thomson had imitated Virgil's lines in 'Spring', ll. 711–25.

Page 19

S) See the first note on Np. 1.

before Winter is expired) the last of the very early entries in the hand of W. W. See above, pp. 3–10.

Soft South wind) Cf. Np. 18.

Page 20

Queries.) The entries in ink on this page appear to be a set of questions to be asked on a tour of the Lake district, presumably the one which D. W. mentions Christopher taking with two schoolfellows in the spring of 1791 (*E.L.*, p. 45).

Did you ever see round rainbows?) Cf. D. W., 30 January 1798: 'William called me into the garden to observe a singular appearance about the moon. A perfect rainbow, within the bow one star, only of colours more vivid. The semi-circle soon became a complete circle, and in the course of three or four minutes the whole faded away' (*Journals*, i. 5).

Dal[t?]on . . . Walney) The ancient town of Dalton-in-Furness and the island off the southwest shore of Furness. The presence of mines in the Lake district and contiguous areas gave rise in past times to various stories of surreptitiously coined and magical pieces of money.

Inserted Leaf 1 *Recto*

I arbitrarily call this the first of the three odd-sized small sheets inserted in the notebook. They all appear to be scraps retrieved from old letters and similar sources. The entries in ink on L1r. are over an illegible mathematical equation in pencil.

Autumn Storm) The numerals refer to numbered entries in the notebook.

Thompson's Seasons) Pages 126–7 of *The Seasons* contain 'Autumn', ll. 311–50, which describe an autumn storm. Pages 148–9 contain 'Autumn', ll. 948–85, which deal with solitary walks in autumn, falling leaves and congregating birds, and an injunction against shooting birds (cf. the last entry on Np. 20). Pages 88–90 contain 'Summer', ll. 1103–60, which detail a destructive storm in late summer. Apparently Christopher looked on the Legberthwaite and St. John's storms referred to on Npp. 1 and 4 as Lake district counterparts of Thomson's. See above, p. 59.

Gilpin) See Np. 4 and note.

Georgics) See Np. 2 and note and L1v.

Mists. Beatties Min. Seasons, 139) See Np. 4 and note. Pages 139–40 of *The Seasons* contain 'Autumn', ll. 705–33.

Description of morning, noon, evening) Cf. Np. 16, the opening passage of *The Vale of Esthwaite*, and 'Septimi Gades', and see above, p. 52.

Storm Lucretius P. 9.) I have not been able to find the work referred to, but the reference must be to Lucretius's description of a destructive storm in ll. 271–94 of *De Rerum Natura*. Apparently this poet's storm and the similar one in Virgil (*Georgics*, i. 316–34) provided Christopher with the classical antecedents for a theme in which he was much interested. According to Bishop Wordsworth, Lucretius was one of the three Latin poets from whom W. W. frequently quoted (*Memoirs*, ii. 482–3).

Spring. Flor. Poet. 14.) *Florilegium Poeticum ex Ovidio, Tibullo, Propertio, Martiali etc., ab omni verborum obscoenitate repurgatum. In usum tyronum*, London, 1714. This anthology, published anonymously, was prepared by G. Whitaker. The description of spring referred to is that in Ovid's *Fasti*, iii. 235–42. Whitaker's collection also contains Ovid's account of Laodamia and Protesilaus in *Heroides*, xiii, to which W. W.'s indebtedness has long been recognized (see Heard in Knight's edition of the *Poet. Wks.*, 1896, vi. 10–14). Was this anthology a schoolbook at Hawkshead?

Ice . . . the striving youth) Cf. Np. 17.

such as I oft have felt on thee oh Esthwaite) Cf. Np. 18.

Fired at the name etc) Cf. Np. 17.

The conduct of the human understanding) Apparently a reference to Locke's posthumously published *The Conduct of the Understanding* or to the more famous *Essay* of which it was intended to be a part.

Leaf 1 *Verso*

Lacuum in Cumbria) Cf. the project for a Latin poem on Np. 2.

Thompson's Seasons) Cf. Np. 11, L1r., and L3r.

Denham. C. Hill) Sir John Denham's 'Cooper's Hill'.

Elegant Ex.) Cf. Np. 4 and note. On p. 4 Thomson's 'Hymn to the Seasons' begins; p. 10 contains Parnell's 'Night Piece on Death' and the beginning of Gray's *Elegy*, with which cf. *V. of Es.*, ll. 456–9. Page 24 includes Miss Carter's 'Written at Midnight in a Thunder Storm' and Mason's 'Elegy on the Death of Lady Coventry'. The opposite page contains Miss Carter's 'Ode to Melancholy', on the relation of which to W. W. see Legouis, *Early Life*, pp. 125–6; and Miss Carter's 'A Night Piece' with the following first line:

While night in solemn shade invests the pole.

This appears to be echoed on Np. 17, where Christopher records that 'night in solemn shade invests the pole'. Page 134 in *Elegant Extracts* contains the beginning of Goldsmith's *The Deserted Village*. The

144

page notation is underlined and the poem is mentioned on L3*r*. in connexion with a description of diversions and sports (cf. also Np. 6). Presumably Christopher had in mind ll. 15–34, with which cf. *Prel.* iv. 272–9 and 316–27 and the Helvellyn fair which opens Book VIII; *The Waggoner*, ii. 30 ff.; and *Excur.* ii. 111–46. Christopher probably also saw the story of the Calgarth skulls (Npp. 13–14) as a Lake district counterpart of Goldsmith's lines

> Amidst thy bowers the tyrant's hand is seen,
> And desolation saddens all the green:
> One only master grasps the whole domain,
> And half a tillage stints thy smiling plain.

Cf. also the 1798 version of the Female Vagrant's story (*Poet. Wks.* i. 108 n.) and see above, pp. 48–50. Moreover, there are thematic analogies between ll. 129–34 of *The Deserted Village* and 'Goody Blake and Harry Gill', and between ll. 325–36 of Goldsmith's poem and the 1800 version of 'The Reverie of Poor Susan'. Page 151 of *Elegant Extracts* contains Mallet's ballad 'Edwin and Emma'; p. 173, underlined, the first part of Dyer's 'Grongar Hill'; p. 208, Parnell's 'Health, an Eclogue', also referred to on L3*r*., and a poem possibly echoed in *The Prelude* (see above, pp. 62–63; p. 221, a passage from Dyer's *The Fleece* praising the simple shepherd life and describing the view from the top of Mount Breaden; p. 225, an extract from Thomson entitled 'Description of a Cataract', with which cf. Np. 2 and note; p. 283, the beginning of Beattie's *The Minstrel*; p. 356, an extract from Thomson headed 'Description of a Man Perishing in the Snow' ('Winter', ll. 276–321), with which cf. Np. 18; p. '356 etc', other selections from *The Seasons*, including the Lavinia story in 'Autumn', ll. 150 f., with which cf. the lines on the Maid of Buttermere in *Prel.* vii. 320–45; p. 489, Rowe's 'The First Feats of a Young Eagle', some lines by Dryden on rural courtship, and under the title 'Description of a Person Left on a Desert Island', Thomson's lines on the abandonment of Melisander in *Agamemnon*, III. i, on which see above, pp. 51–52; p. 383, *The Merchant of Venice*, v. i. 1–24, under the title 'Description of a Moon-light Night with Fine Music'; p. 387, Puck's speech in *Midsummer Night's Dream*, v. 378–97.

Ode pop. supersti. Lucretius etc Georgics) Cf. the reference to the 'Ode' on Np. 13 and see note; that to Lucretius on L1*r*., and see note; and that to the *Georgics*, Np. 2 and see note.

Leaf 2 *Recto* and *Verso*

The only one of the three inserted sheets which appears to have no relation in subject-matter to the rest of the notebook. The *recto* clearly consists of a school exercise and the *verso* either is part of an old letter or a prose composition with an interwritten Latin distich.

Leaf 3 *Recto*

This page appears to be mostly a tabulation of themes in the series of numbered entries in the notebook. There is a close correlation between the numerals, the words above them, and the numbered entries, the only deviation being in the case of the crossed out numeral 3.

Thompson's Seasons, P. 186) Contains 'Winter', ll. 596–624, of which ll. 617–24 deal with tales of the supernatural told on winter evenings and the beginning of the lines on a rural dance which provide a striking analogue with *Prel.* iv. 316–27.

a digression, at Callgarth) See above, pp. 20–21, Npp. 13–14 and notes.

Deserted Village) See the note to the reference to *Elegant Extracts* on L1v.

Health Eleg. Ex. 208) Cf. L1v. and note.

Pastoral life. T. Seasons, 158, 175, 157, 158) Page 158 contains 'Autumn', ll. 1222–32 on seasonal festivities, and ll. 1233–52 in praise of the simple rural life. Page 175 has 'Winter', ll. 281–310, which contain most of the account of a man perishing in the snow which is related to an entry on Np. 18 (see also note). Page 157 contains 'Autumn', ll. 1192–1221, the last three of which contain the beginning of the passage on autumn festivals referred to above.

Skiddaw. Grongar Hill) Cf. Np. 15 and note. Dyer's poem appears on p. 176, one of the underscored pages of *Elegant Extracts* referred to on L1v. See also the note to 'Oft Hd. have I heard' on Np. 17. W. W. had a continuing admiration for Dyer, asserting on one occasion that he was not sure that Dyer was not the superior in imagination to any poet since Milton (*M.Y.*, p. 478). See also in addition to the well-known sonnet to Dyer, *L.Y.*, p. 346, W.'s notes to *The River Duddon*, and his note to *Excur.* viii. 111–12.

Apostrophe to the river Derwent) See above, pp. 25–26.

Leaf 3 *Verso*

This sheet was apparently retrieved from the unused portion of an old letter, for the date 1771 in ink and in a hand wholly different from any other in the notebook appears along the edge at the right and at right angles to the later entries in ink. Then the sheet was used to work out a still legible equation in pencil, no doubt a school exercise, to which Christopher's entries in ink were afterwards made at right angles. The itinerary in the prose synopsis which they contain, involving well-known points of interest in the Lake district, clearly represents a stage in the ordering of materials for Christopher's projected topographical poem which lies somewhere between the entries in the notebook proper and the 'Outline of a Poem descriptive of the lakes', with which it is very closely connected (see p. 148). Cf. also Gray's account in the *Journal* of his visit to the same area (West's *Guide*, pp. 203–5):

A heavenly day; rose at seven, and walked out under the conduct of my landlord to Borrowdale; the grass was covered with a hoar-frost, which soon melted and exhaled in a thin bluish smoke. . . . A little farther, passing a brook called Barrow Beck, we entered Borrowdale; the crags named Lowdore-Banks begin now to impend terribly over the way [here follows the description of the crags that fell referred to on Np. 5]. . . . Here we met a civil young farmer overseeing his reapers (for it is now oat harvest) who conducted us to a neat white house in the village of Grange, which is built on a rising ground in the midst of a valley; round it the mountains form an awful amphitheatre, and through it obliquely runs the Derwent, clear as glass, and shewing under its bridge every trout that passes. . . . The wood of the mountains encreases, and their summits grow loftier to the eye, and of more fantastic forms; among them appear Eagle's-Cliff, Dove's-Nest, Whitedale-Pike etc. celebrated names in the annals of Keswick. . . . The dale opens about four miles higher . . . all farther access is here barred to prying mortals, only there is a little path winding over the fells, and for some weeks in the year passable to the dalesmen; but the mountains know well that these innocent people will not reveal the mysteries of their ancient kingdom. . . . For me, I went no further than the farmer's (better than four miles from Keswick) at Grange; his mother and he brought us butter that Siserah would have jumped at, though not in a lordly dish, bowls of milk, thin oaten-cakes, and ale, and we had carried a cold tongue thither with us [here follows the account of the robbing of an eagle's nest referred to on Np. 2].

This same passage, obviously Christopher's inspiration, was also Dorothy's in a letter which she wrote when she was at Windy Brow with William (see *E.L.*, pp. 111–12). On its relation to W. W. see above, pp. 67–68.

Morning. Mist. (not the elaborate description)) For what Christopher had in mind by the elaborate description see Np. 4 and note.

To Crommack. Scaleforce etc.) Descriptions of both Crummock Water and Scale Force, later omitted, are found in the first version of W. W.'s *Guide* (see de Selincourt's edition, p. 169).

Apostrophe to that river) See L3r. and note.

but alas! in life nothing is to be enjoyed long) Cf. *D.S.*, l. 636:

Soon flies the little joy to man allowed,

and W. W.'s note citing *Optima quaeque dies* etc. (*Georgics*, iii. 66–68.)

II. NOTES TO 'OUTLINE OF A POEM'

On the dating of the 'Outline', its relation to the notebook, and Christopher's motives in writing it, see above, pp. 10–11, 104.

The plan calls for an itinerary poem based on two routes. The first runs by the estates of Dalemain and Watermillock, noted for their views in Christopher's day, past the conical hill of Dunmallet at the foot of Ullswater, and thence by Gowbarrow Park, Lyulph's Tower, Aira Force, Glencoin, and Patterdale, all points of interest in the Ullswater region, over Kirkstone Pass to Ambleside and then back again—essentially the road between Penrith and Ambleside as it existed in the late eighteenth century and as it appears on the map prefixed to various editions of West's *Guide*. The second route, starting again from Penrith, follows the road to Keswick by way of Threlkeld, and proceeds by the roads out of Keswick to Borrowdale, Bassenthwaite, Newlands, Buttermere, Crummock Water, Lowes Water, and Scale Force. An ascent of Skiddaw and the view from that mountain were also to be included. Then, again from Keswick, the route follows the Ambleside road past Legberthwaite Valley, Thirlmere, Dunmail Raise, Grasmere, and Rydal. From Ambleside it proceeds to Windermere and Esthwaite Water, with a eulogy on which the poem was to close.

A friend who is thought of as accompanying Christopher is several times addressed. Though such references were a convention of the loco-descriptive poem—cf. William's use of the same device in *E.W.*, ll. 1 and 51)—the suggestion is that an actual person was in mind. Possibly he was one of the two schoolfellows mentioned by D. W., as accompanying Christopher on the walking tour of the Lake district in the spring of 1791 (*E.L.*, p. 45). In this case he may have been either Atkinson or Leeson, apparently schoolboys, referred to on Np. 9. He was evidently not H., probably also a schoolboy, who is mentioned on pp. 105 and 118, and who was a nephew of John Robinson, Esq., of Watermillock.

Since the 'Outline' and the notebook cover much of the same material, to avoid repetition I have used cross-references to matters already treated.

Page 104

Ille terrarum mihi) *Carmina*, II. vi. 13–14.

I sing lakes, woods & mountains) Cf. Np. 2.

148

Page 105

Gowbarrow Park) Cf. Np. 6 and note.

Page 106

specus adverso sole) Cf. *Aeneid*, iv. 701.

Lucretius, P. 115) Not in Whitaker's *Florilegium Poeticum*, referred to on p. 111 and L1r., but probably a reference to a similar anthology. Doubtless Christopher had in mind *De Rerum Natura*, iv. 221.

Page 107

Here reigns the king of patterdale) Cf. Np. 2 and note.

Mosedale beck inundation) The same storm as that in St. John's Vale, referred to on Npp. 1 and 4 (see notes).

Southerfell rebellion sights) Cf. Np. 14 and notes and pp. 29–32.

Thomp. Seasons, 154) This page contains 'Autumn', ll. 1106–35, Thomson's treatment of the theme of armies in the sky. Cf. Np. 14 and note and pp. 29–32.

Page 108

let us betake ourselves to the shore of the lake) Cf. the description of the evening in Gray's *Journal to the Lakes* as printed on p. 206 of West's *Guide*, referred to on Np. 5.

Even now while the shades of evening are advancing) Cf. Np. 17 and the concluding lines of *E.W.*, particularly ll. 433–46.

Page 109

We will set out . . . for Borrowdale) Cf. L3v.

See Eleg. Ext. P. 225) Also referred to on L1v., and see note. It contains Thomson's description of a cataract in 'Summer', ll. 585–606.

We enter Borrowdale under rocks threatening to crush) Cf. Np. 5.

Page 110

Taking of eagle's eyrie) Cf. Np. 2 and note.

Page 111

In wrestling, cudgelling) Cf. Np. 6.

Their character, give them exactly the same as Goldsmith) Cf. *The Traveller*, ll. 175–98:

> Yet still, even here, content can spread a charm,
> Redress the clime, and all its rage disarm.
> Though poor the peasant's hut, his feasts though small,
> He sees his little lot the lot of all;
> Sees no contiguous palace rear its head
> To shame the meanness of his humble shed;
> No costly lord the sumptuous banquet deal
> To make him loathe his vegetable meal;
> But calm, and bred in ignorance and toil,
> Each wish contracting, fits him to the soil.
> Chearful at morn, he wakes from short repose,
> Breasts the keen air, and carrols as he goes;
> With patient angle trolls the finny deep,
> Or drives his venturous plowshare to the steep;
> Or seeks the den where snow-tracks mark the way,
> And drags the struggling savage into day.
> At night returning, every labour sped,
> He sits him down the monarch of a shed;
> Smiles by his chearful fire, and round surveys
> His childrens looks, that brighten at the blaze;
> While his lov'd partner, boastful of her hoard,
> Displays her cleanly platter on the board;
> And haply, too, some pilgrim thither led,
> With many a tale repays the nightly bed.

Flor. Poet. 54) Cf. L1r., on which this school anthology is also referred to, and see note. Page 54 contains Tibullus, *Carmina*, ii. i. 37–70, on the rural gods who weaned man from his primeval savage fare and taught him the simple rural life.

These seen ni piget I would carry you through various excursions) Cf. L3v.

Clarke, p. 55) Refers to the account of the Southerfell horsemen in Clarke's *Survey of the Lakes*. Cf. Npp. 14 and 12 and notes.

Page 112

P. 57) Clarke's account of the great storm of 1749, referred to on Npp. 1 and 4, and in the 'Outline' earlier on p. 107.

Skiddaw) Cf. Np. 15.

Page 113

Along the side of the Derwent) Cf. L3r. and v.

We must leave, my Friend these delicious scenes) Cf. L3v.

Page 114

Flor. Poet. 71) Contains Ovid, *Fasti*, iv. 419–38, on the rape of Proserpine.

Page 115

Morning. Noon and Evening) Cf. Np. 17.

At the approach of spring) Cf. Npp. 18, 7.

Flor. Poet. 14) Ovid, *Fasti*, iii. 235–42, also referred to on L1r.

In summer how delightful) Cf. Np. 17.

In autumn. In the morning) Cf. Np. 4 and notes.

In autumn too, livid sky in the east) Cf. Np. 10 and pp. 157 and 161–2 and notes.

aridus fragor) *Georgics*, i. 357–8.

Page 116

Storm Lucretius page 9th) Cf. L1r. and note.

Georg. 1.) A reference to the storm in *Georgics*, i. 316–34.

In Winter. Snow sleet) Cf. Np. 17.

Addison's poem) Cf. Np. 17 and note.

such as I have often felt) Cf. Np. 18 and L1r.

Fired with the) Cf. Np. 17 and L1r.

chiefly eminent for an ancient and respected seminary) Cf. Np. 2.

[?] tenues haustus) Cf. Hor. *Epist.* i. iii. 10.

Page 117

Here oft with impatience I have watched) Cf. Np. 17.

Then oft when the sky was contracting) Cf. Np. 18.

Thus have I wandered along the lake) Cf. Npp. 17 and 1.

tacitae per amica silentia lunae) *Aeneid*, ii. 255.

In summer, hid from day's garish eye) Cf. Np. 17.

Page 118

For me whithersoever the stream of life may carry me) Cf. *V. of Es.*, ll. 498–507, and *Prel.*, 1850, viii. 468–75.

H.) See above, p. 148.

INDEX

153

154

THE EARLY
WORDSWORTHIAN
MILIEU

Oxford University Press, Amen House, London E.C.4

GLASGOW NEW YORK TORONTO MELBOURNE WELLINGTON
BOMBAY CALCUTTA MADRAS KARACHI KUALA LUMPUR
CAPE TOWN IBADAN NAIROBI ACCRA

His vapour glittered in the
but fear sat on his forehead, or when
the sun shoots his beams upon
the side of Skiddaw or Helvellyn
but mists settle upon his head.

avid avid love

1 Storm at Legberthwaite.
sultry day, Autumn, August, ? Oct
evening thunder lightning, rain
Helvellyn. vast stones.

2 Evening the sound of the torrent
the whirring & quaking of the greys
duck.
3 oft have I have walked till the
golden ways in the west fade
into the other gray of the
evening, & even till twilight
4 Description of a vale upon
Windermere by day.
or drawn by night. Cont

Notebook, page 1